TURN CALLS INTO CUSTOMERS

Maximize Customer Experience With Your Call Center

Judith A. Brown

HealthLeaders Media
A Division of HCPro

HCPro

Turn Calls into Customers: Maximize Customer Experience with Your Call Center is published by HCPro, Inc.

Copyright © 2008 HCPro, Inc.

All rights reserved. Printed in the United States of America.   5 4 3 2 1

ISBN 978-1-60146-190-2

No part of this publication may be reproduced, in any form or by any means, without prior written consent of HCPro, Inc., or the Copyright Clearance Center (978/750-8400). Please notify us immediately if you have received an unauthorized copy.

HCPro, Inc., provides information resources for the healthcare industry.

HCPro, Inc., is not affiliated in any way with The Joint Commission, which owns the JCAHO and Joint Commission trademarks.

Judith A. Brown, Author
Maureen O. Larkin, Managing Editor
Amy Anthony, Executive Editor
Matthew Cann, Group Publisher
Doug Ponte, Cover Designer
Jackie Diehl Singer, Graphic Artist

David Lundgren, Copyeditor
Amanda Donaldson, Proofreader
Darren Kelly, Books Production
Susan Darbyshire, Art Director
Jean St. Pierre, Director of Operations
Paul Singer, Layout Artist

Advice given is general. Readers should consult professional counsel for specific legal, ethical, or clinical questions.

Arrangements can be made for quantity discounts. For more information, contact:

HCPro, Inc.
P.O. Box 1168
Marblehead, MA 01945
Telephone: 800/650-6787 or 781/639-1872
Fax: 781/639-2982
E-mail: *customerservice@hcpro.com*

Visit HCPro at its World Wide Web sites:
www.hcpro.com and *www.hcmarketplace.com*

06/2008
21456

Contents

Chapter 1: The history of hospital-based call centers: An introduction 1
    Rolodex referrals 3
    Changing times 4
    Nurse telephone triage returns 6
    Technology brings changes 6
    A bit about me 7

Chapter 2: Customer interaction: Why the basics are essential 11
    Avoid the ping-pong game 14
    Hiring the right representatives 14
    Marketers must be involved 19
    Collaboration 19
    Communication 21
    Clarity 22
    Cooperation 22
    It's about the basics 23

Chapter 3: Consumerism and the new healthcare consumer 25
    Early adopters of consumerism? 28
    Consumers looking for information 28
    Time to start the dialogue 32
    Answering consumers' questions 32
    Ahead of the curve? 34
    Circling back to customer service 35

Contents

Chapter 4: Cross-selling at its best 37
    Three ways to cross-sell 40
    Structured and streamlined cross-selling 42
    It's not all good 44

Chapter 5: Make vs. buy 47
    Analyze your situation 50
    Determine its purpose 51
    What will your call center provide? 51
    Cost vs. revenue 52
    The bottom line 53
    A true comparison 53
    If you outsource 56

Chapter 6: Demonstrating credible ROI to the C-suite 59
    Four call center models 62
    Know what your organization wants 64
    Tracking ROI: A necessary step 69

Chapter 7: CRM comes to healthcare: Stories from other industries 71
    CRM: Part of a bigger strategy 75
    Not just software 76
    Customer experience management 76
    It's okay to start small 77

Chapter 8: Case studies and best practices in clinical services integration 79
    Managing children's asthma care 83
    Asthma assistance a phone call away 84

Introducing the program to the physician community 84
Results..85
Cleveland Clinic 85
Clinical research at the call center 87
Emory's call center prescreens 89
AtlantiCare..90
Determining your approach 91

Chapter 9: Moving beyond marketing into hospital operations: Touch points along the patient continuum 93

Expansion isn't an experiment 95
Helping patients beat traffic..97
Emory helps its employees 98
A way to show strengths, weaknesses 99
Mystery shopping..100
A virtual front door 101

Chapter 10: Embrace transparency, empower your customers, and build your business.. 105

We've got the technology, and they know it 108
More progress to make 108
Map out the customer experience 109
'Mega' call centers..110
Web integration..111
Physician relations and the call center..112
Outside the hospital 114
Final thoughts 115

Acknowledgments

There are so many people to thank who provided support, insight, and critique during the writing of this book. There are also the countless marketing and call center colleagues with whom I have had the distinct opportunity to have worked with and learned from over the years. Individuals cross our lives and influence us in ways that shape our perspectives and thinking and, as a result, broaden our knowledge and enable us to learn.

Several individuals have been instrumental with this publication that I would like to specifically thank. First, I'd like to thank HealthLeaders Media for the chance to write this book, highlighting the role of the healthcare call center. I want to thank Maureen O. Larkin, managing editor, for her guidance, which kept the project running smoothly and on schedule.

Heartfelt thanks are extended to Rick Stier, vice president of HealthLine Systems, Inc., for his generosity in sharing his time, knowledge, and resources. He graciously took all of my calls, listened to ideas, and offered critiques.

I am also indebted to the many healthcare leaders who contributed to this book in their case studies. None of the individuals featured in this book needed to take the time to be interviewed, reply to phone calls and e-mails, and review drafts. However, their commitment to this book shows their dedication to this industry and their vision to see call centers grow and flourish within healthcare providers.

Acknowledgments

I am also grateful to the many call center representatives with whom I have had the distinct pleasure to work with over the past 20 years. I have learned a great deal from their interactions with callers. It made me a better marketer and a better manager. I would encourage any marketing professional to spend time in the call center listening to calls and learning about the customer firsthand.

I would also like to thank Leann Delaney, director, regional sales for LVM Systems, Jonathan Fine, and Valerie White for providing whatever assistance I needed whenever I asked.

To my family, I would like to thank my parents for instilling a spirit of a strong work ethic and the idea that anything is possible. And to my son Michael, thank you for your fun-loving, generous spirit that brightens our lives. And to my husband, Mark, thank you for your unwavering confidence, love, and patience. I love you all.

About the author

Judith A. Brown has worked in the healthcare industry for more than two decades with a diverse background of experiences as a registered nurse, provider executive, and consultant. Currently a healthcare consultant, Brown works with hospitals and hospital marketing vendors in the areas of marketing plan development, customer contact mapping, call center consulting and implementation, and business operations.

Previously, Brown was the vice president of corporate, government, and consumer relations at Advocate Health Care in Oak Brook, IL. She was responsible for business-to-business marketing and sales, occupational medicine, fitness and wellness services, government relations, contact center operations, consumer Internet, and enterprise data warehouse management and customer relationship management strategy. Prior to joining Advocate, Brown was with Northwestern Memorial Hospital in Chicago, where she led the team that started the organization's first call center. Her clinical roots are also tied to Northwestern, where she was in nursing management before transitioning to marketing.

A featured speaker at a variety of national healthcare organizations and conferences, Brown has served on numerous advisory boards. She is also involved in community volunteerism and continues to clinically practice. Brown is a graduate of Michigan State University in East Lansing, and resides in suburban Chicago.

Dedication

This book is dedicated in loving memory to Georgeanne Pellettieri.

An exceptional contact center leader
A respected colleague
A good friend

1

The history of hospital-based call centers: An introduction

CHAPTER 1

The history of hospital-based call centers: An introduction

Hospital-based call centers have a lot in common with each other, yet each one maintains its own unique history and experiences. The commonalities are the foundation upon which most of today's hospital-based call centers are built. Some started as a nurse triage service—an outgrowth of a service provided in the hospital emergency department. Others started as physician referral services, with their roots in medical staff offices or admitting departments. And still others have their roots in community education—the departments that plan, coordinate, and teach health classes to the community.

Rolodex referrals

If you've been around the hospital call center industry since the 1980s, you've seen quite an evolution. When they first started, call centers weren't known as such and, in most cases, they weren't computerized. Many call centers had only one or two highly knowledgeable staff members who provided information about the hospital's services and physicians to people calling in from the

Chapter 1

community. This information was often stored in a staff member's head or in a Rolodex—the early version of a physician referral and health information service.

These individuals often gave highly personalized attention to the callers, but if they were out sick or away from their desks, the call center was left without coverage, and customer needs went unmet. At the time, hospital marketing was just getting started, and the idea of viewing patients as customers was only in its infancy. There wasn't much interest in making the hospital call center into something more sophisticated.

Changing times

Managed care, physicians wanting to grow their practices, and an expansion of hospital marketing changed the purpose of the hospital call center. Providing consumers with information was still an important part of a call center representative's job, but the scope of information that a call center could provide had outgrown the small-staff model of the early call center.

It was impossible for a single person to keep track of all the information that a call center must be able to provide customers. One person was unable to memorize every managed care plan that each hospital physician participated in. Running a hospital call center had become a more complex process, as callers had an expectation that the hospital would be able to refer them to a physician who participated in their health plan.

The history of hospital-based call centers: An introduction

Physicians were increasingly concerned about receiving their fair share of referrals. Consequently, they wanted call centers to keep updated information about which insurance plans were accepted by their offices and for which of those plans they were accepting new patients.

Increased hospital marketing also affected the hospital call center. Each new marketing initiative launched by the hospital increased the number of calls coming in from members of the community. Because more staff members were needed to answer the increased calls, gone were the days when all the necessary information could be held by one person.

Thus began the evolution of the hospital call center, and it wasn't long before contact-management software and basic call center telephonic systems made their way into the hospital.

For many hospitals, physician referral and general organizational information were the cornerstones of their call center services. For some, that is still the case today. Many began to add class and event registration capabilities in the 1980s and 1990s to provide direct response for marketing offers. Some call centers also expanded to provide fulfillment of marketing offers, such as first-aid kits and new movers' packages, which offered a single point of contact for the customer calling the healthcare organization.

CHAPTER 1

Nurse telephone triage returns

In the 1990s, one of the biggest changes to many hospital call centers was the revamping of nurse telephone triage. Although nurse telephone triage had been around for more than a decade, some organizations were now using the service as a marketing initiative. For many organizations, telephone triage came on the scene hand in hand with the introduction of managed care plans that were full-risk capitation. The provider was now fully responsible for ensuring that members received the right care, at the right time, and at the right place. Computer-based protocols, or algorithms, were developed, and nurses were trained in how to telephonically guide callers through an assessment and advise them on the level of care they should seek—ranging from calling 911 to practicing self care.

As managed care has changed, the hospital call center has evolved. Many organizations no longer broadly market nurse telephone triage, but have targeted their initiatives into areas of support for hospital clinical operations and physician practices.

Technology brings changes

Not only have the services delivered by the hospital call center changed over the past two decades, but so have the vehicles for delivering information to the consumer. The Internet is one such vehicle, giving customers the ability to acquire information about an organization and potentially interact with it. In some hospitals, this interaction is managed by the call center, thus transforming this entity yet again into something slightly different—a "contact center."

The history of hospital-based call centers: An introduction

Many hospital contact centers today are engaging in the management of e-mail, online chat services, and other Internet-based interactions. The terms "call center" and "contact center" are often used interchangeably in the industry. However, the call center is generally an inbound and outbound telephonic entity, where as the contact center manages inbound and outbound correspondence of all types—telephonic, Internet, and direct mail fulfillment–response management.

A bit about me

My career with call centers started in the early 1990s, when I was asked to create a database marketing center at Northwestern Memorial Hospital in Chicago, an 897-bed academic medical center with 1,545 physicians on the medical staff. Although at the time I wasn't sure exactly what this meant, it sounded like a new challenge and a great opportunity for learning—which have been the basis for most of my career decisions. I did not know I would be starting a call center. I couldn't have even told you at the time what a call center was. And so my own journey began.

Up until that point, Northwestern offered a physician referral service, but had decentralized access points for all other consumer contacts. During my tenure there, we began using a single phone number for customers to contact the hospital. Using a centralized database, this single-point-of-contact system allowed us to:

Chapter 1

- Receive and track all inbound marketing calls
- Provide physician referrals
- Assist patients with scheduling physician office appointments
- Register consumers for classes and events
- Screen candidates for clinical trials

With the systems we put in place, Northwestern was now able to track contribution margin for marketing campaigns, complete analytics on campaign responders, and produce outbound direct mail campaigns to targeted customer groups using the data collected via the call center.

In the mid-1990s, I had the opportunity to join what is now Advocate Health Care, the largest integrated healthcare delivery system in metropolitan Chicago, with 3,500 beds, eight hospitals, and 4,600 physicians. While I was at Advocate, its call center grew from receiving 38,000 calls per year to making more than 350,000 contacts per year, while adding a new hospital or large physician group to the system every year. The foundation for physician referral and event registration was already in place at Advocate when I joined the organization. However, as this integrated delivery system grew, it provided an environment to deploy inbound and outbound call center tactics, including:

- Childhood immunization reminder calls
- New member welcome and health screening calls for Medicare managed care enrollees
- Online physician appointment requests

The history of hospital-based call centers: An introduction

- Event registrations
- Nurse telephone triage
- Disease management for congestive heart failure patients
- Crisis communication

The diversity of the system enabled the call center to create new services to meet the needs of a growing and changing organization that hoped to serve several unique patient populations.

As I reflect on more than 20 years in hospital call centers and remember the first time I sat down with one of those knowledgeable staff members and her Rolodex to learn how to provide a physician referral, I have to acknowledge that the industry has come a long way. Yet with the demands of today's healthcare consumer, the changing healthcare marketplace, and the abundance of healthcare information available today, the future is filled with tremendous opportunities for the hospital contact center.

Customer interaction: Why the basics are essential

Chapter 2

Customer interaction: Why the basics are essential

Marketers may be inclined to skip this chapter, thinking that customer interaction is the responsibility of the call center manager and representatives answering the phone. But to really achieve the optimal customer experience, marketers must play a role.

Ideally, through the effective use of marketing and public relations channels, customers will know how to reach your hospital's contact center. A news story, radio spot, or television advertisement will prompt consumers to seek out your organization's call center, and thus make a direct connection with a call center representative. But this doesn't always happen. To make sure your customers always have an optimal experience, a marketer must realize that a customer's experience with your hospital begins long before the call center representative answers the phone.

CHAPTER 2

Avoid the ping-pong game

The seconds or minutes preceding the connection with a call center representative can often explain the state the customer is in when the conversation is initiated. For example, callers who have been transferred multiple times before getting to the call center may be frustrated and feel like a ping-pong ball being volleyed about. Another less-than-ideal experience is being placed on hold while waiting for a call center representative. Depending on the length of time customers have been on hold, they may express anger or frustration once connected to a representative. They may also reach a breaking point and abandon the call, only to redial and be put on hold again. One of the greatest complaints about call centers is an automated attendant with a multilayer menu that stands between a customer and a live representative.

Each one of these scenarios presents unique challenges for the call center manager. Working collaboratively with marketing colleagues, the manager must facilitate clear direct response consumer communication, manage staffing resources to minimize hold times and abandoned call rates, and minimize the use of automated attendant menus for call routing.

Hiring the right representatives

Regardless of how the customer gets through to the call center—whether through the ideal scenario or not—it is the representative's role to create a positive, "wow" experience for the customer. In some cases, more than 60% of a contact center's callers are new to the organization, making that phone call the first time the customer experiences the hospital or health system. These calls are opportunities for your organization to create a positive first impression with new customers or build its relationship with repeat customers.

Just as the customer's experience doesn't start when the call is answered, ensuring that customers are wowed doesn't start with training—it starts with hiring. During the hiring process, candidates should be interviewed for their customer-service ability. Some organizations have their human resources department screen potential candidates with assessment instruments—a sort of standardized test that allows them to measure a candidate's ability to provide exceptional customer service. Although this may be helpful in establishing a baseline for the manager, further probing is critical considering that a representative's role involves talking virtually nonstop with consumers. Hiring managers must evaluate the candidate's ability to converse with a caller who needs assistance in navigating the healthcare system or whose family member is in a health crisis.

In the hiring process, call center managers need to implement experiential or performance interviewing techniques to determine how candidates would handle various customer scenarios—e.g., "Describe a situation when a customer was angry and how you responded." Listen to their tone of voice and the words they use. One of the particularly challenging aspects of the call center environment is that voice and word choice are the primary vehicles for communication. Ask yourself:

Chapter 2

- How do they convey an empathetic response or a listening response through the phone?
- How do they convey their smile through the phone?

Savvy call center managers have learned how to interview for these skills and provide ongoing training, either through in-house resources or external experts specializing in call center environments.

AtlantiCare uses team-based interviewing in the selection process for call center representatives. Behavioral interview questions are asked of candidates, and the interviewing team uses a scorecard to gather perceptions, compile results, and discuss the outcomes. "We have been very fortunate in hiring staff," says Maureen Donzuso, contact center manager. The contact center has had no turnover in the past two years, which is exceptional in an industry where turnover often exceeds 25% annually.

About AtlantiCare

AtlantiCare, located in New Jersey, includes AtlantiCare Regional Medical Center (ARMC), AtlantiCare Health Services, AtlantiCare Behavioral Health, AtlantiCare Foundation, and AtlantiCare Health Plans. AtlantiCare is the region's largest healthcare organization and non-casino employer. ARMC is a 567-bed teaching hospital with campuses in Atlantic City, NJ, and Pomona, NJ.

www.atlanticare.org

Interview Questions

During the selection process of new staff members, AtlantiCare uses the scorecard in Figure 2.1, as well as the following interview questions:

- What specific goals, including those related to your career or occupation, have you established?
- What influenced you to pursue this position?
- What motivates you to put forth your greatest effort?
- Given the investment our company will make in hiring and training you, can you give us a reason to hire you?
- Have you ever had difficulty with a supervisor or instructor? How did you resolve the conflict?
- What personal weakness has caused you the greatest difficulty in school or on the job?
- Have you ever been able to persuade someone to see things your way? Provide examples.
- Has a situation ever tested your coping skills? Provide examples.
- What kind of supervisor do you work best for? Provide examples.
- What was your most difficult customer-service experience, what did you do, and what was the outcome?

Figure 2.1 AtlanticCare Interview Scorecard

Name:_____   Date:_____

	Excellent (3)	Average (2)	Below average (1)	Total
Technical skills				
PC skills				
Typing skills				
Healthcare experience				
Communication skills				
Tone and diction				
Ability to sell				
Patience				
Level of listening skills				
Ability to size up people and situations				
Written				
Behavioral team fit				
Reliability				
Longevity				
Sense of humor				
Willingnesss to help others				
Detail Oriented				
Ability to handle stress or fast-paced environment				
Receptivity to feedback, supervision and authority				
Total Score				

Marketers must be involved

I've established that the call center manager's work begins before a single call is answered, but managers aren't the only ones working behind the scenes to create a "wow" experience for the customer. Marketers must also ensure the desired consumer effect is achieved before the ads are placed and the direct mail pieces mailed.

In talking with hospital call center and marketing leaders across the United States, four characteristics of high-performing teams have consistently been highlighted:

- Collaboration
- Communication
- Clarity
- Cooperation

Collaboration

Collaboration between call center and marketing teams is critical. Ideally, this is a recurring process that takes place as campaigns and marketing tactics are in development. I recall working with an organization where the marketing and call center teams had not historically collaborated together. One of the marketing tactics was to mail a quarterly community newsletter to more than 750,000 households. The call center staff received a copy of the publication the same day it was mailed to the households.

Although one could argue that the call center was being communicated with, there were missed opportunities for collaboration. By changing the process to have the call center staff members involved with the editorial review, they were able to verify the dates and times of calls to action, availability of fulfillment items, addresses of event locations, and a multitude of other items that, when left unverified, diminished the call center's ability to create an exceptional customer experience.

Call center representatives are also the voice of the customer. "Consulting with the call center staff can provide valuable insight as to how consumers may perceive something," says Lori McLelland, executive director of marketing for Emory Healthcare in Atlanta. McLelland is also responsible for Emory's call center, which handles 200,000 calls annually.

> **About Emory HealthCare**
>
> Emory HealthCare is the largest, most comprehensive health system in Georgia. It has 1,184 licensed patient beds, 9,000 employees, and more than 20 health centers located throughout metropolitan Atlanta. In 2007, the call center received 200,000 calls. In addition to clinical-trial screening, the Emory call center provides physician referrals for consumers and physicians, class and event registration, referrals to Emory services, collection of data, statistical analysis, and other services.
>
> *www.emoryhealthcare.org*

I encountered a perfect example of this while managing a call center. The marketing staff had marketed a call to action that offered a free book to respondents. There was a narrative description of the book in the ad, yet, after the direct mail piece was sent, there was virtually no response. One of the senior call center representatives suggested that the hospital try the same mailing again, but with a picture of the book in addition to the narrative description. The call center representative thought the picture would appeal to consumers, and she was right. With the next mailing, the book sold out.

Communication

Communication is the next key characteristic of high-performing collaborative marketing and call center teams, and it is critical to ensuring that customers are serviced well. With regular communication and careful planning, the two departments can schedule when various marketing initiatives will hit the airwaves, Web site, or mailboxes. This can have an enormous effect on the ability of the call center representatives to provide positive customer interaction and create that outstanding first impression. If everything is dropping at the same time, it is setting your organization up for a failed campaign before the first call comes in.

Lost calls negatively affect an organization's return on investment. With effective communication and advance planning, call center managers can adjust staffing resources and other projects to better ensure higher service levels and reduced abandoned call rates. Yet even with the best-laid plans, the unexpected happens, so getting information to your call center staff quickly is critical. "You never want to lose the confidence of the caller by the call center staff being unprepared," McLelland says.

Clarity

Both call center managers and marketers have roles to play in ensuring that callers receive clear messages and information from the facility. Messages and calls to action should be simple and direct. Customers become frustrated and will be easily discouraged from pursuing an offer if they find it too complicated to understand. Being clear with consumers about what you want them to do is critical. Keep it simple. If the action is to make a call to the contact center, then try to have the call come in to a live person. Although that isn't always possible, ensure that the use of an automated attendant is kept to a minimum and that multilayer menus are avoided.

Cooperation

The fourth key principle that will ensure a positive customer interaction is cooperation between marketing and the call center. Either entity working independently can position the other to fail.

Call center staff members should preview marketing plans, collateral material, advertisements, and press releases—anything that is leaving your organization for public viewing. Training of the call center staff should not be left solely to the call center manager. For example, if call center representatives will field calls about particular programs or services, it may make sense to have staff members involved in those programs conduct training. They put a face to the program and often feel passionate about the initiative with which they are engaged, thus instilling an extra sense of enthusiasm into the call center representative.

Julie Bruns, director of call center and market research at BJC HealthCare in St. Louis, characterized this as a "can-do," positive attitude. Teams that are creative and strive to find ways to create memorable moments for customers are the ones that will achieve repeat callers and loyalty.

About BJC HealthCare
BJC HealthCare is one of the largest nonprofit healthcare organizations in the United States. It is located in St. Louis and serves residents throughout that area, including southern Illinois and the mid-Missouri regions. The system has 13 hospitals, 3,508 staffed beds, and multiple community-health locations. The organization provides inpatient and outpatient care, primary care, community health and wellness, workplace health, home health, community mental health, rehabilitation, long-term care, and hospice. BJC's contact center has an annual call volume of 500,000 and provides the following services:

- Physician referral
- Class and event registration
- Campaign fulfillment
- After-hours pediatric triage and pediatrician answering service
- Consult line
- Database development/CRM
- Wait-time studies
- Event follow-up calls
- Patient satisfaction measurement

www.bjc.org

It's about the basics

Customer interaction is truly about the basics. If each member of the team is committed to a common goal of providing experiences in which customers will be delighted, then your customers will experience the result of the four Cs: collaboration, communication, clarity, and cooperation.

Chapter 2

Do not underestimate the role of exceptional customer service, whether it is at the bedside or in an exchange with the caller seeking a physician referral. Consumers are seeking and expecting exceptional service from their healthcare provider. As the new healthcare consumer emerges, customers will be seeking cost and quality information about your organization and contacting your hospital if they are unable to find or understand the information they are looking for. They may increasingly turn to customer service as the competitive differentiator as they make healthcare decisions for themselves and their families.

Consumerism and the new healthcare consumer

Chapter 3

Consumerism and the new healthcare consumer

It is nearly impossible today to pick up a healthcare publication—or even a newspaper or weekly news magazine—and not see articles about the movement toward consumerism in healthcare. There are public and private initiatives under way to expand this movement further, forcing it into the national spotlight.

Some would argue that consumerism is not a new healthcare trend, but an old one simply being revisited, as many trends are. Prior to managed care, consumers paid for a much larger portion of their healthcare expenses—particularly outpatient expenses. Physician office visits, most outpatient care, and prescriptions were items largely paid for by consumers. Although consumers may not have been calling around looking for the lowest price, the issue of actual prescription costs vs. a flat copayment amount didn't exist 50 years ago.

Even though price may have been more obvious to consumers prior to managed care, there are two new consumer characteristics that didn't exist in the

Chapter 3

pre–managed care era: a focus on the quality of care and exceptional customer service. Consumers expect a hospital to make cost, quality, and customer-service information available in a way that is meaningful, reliable, relevant, and timely.

Early adopters of consumerism?

Physician referral service veterans might contend that those calling physician referral services in the 1980s were early adopters of healthcare consumerism. They were consumers looking for credible information—some of which was not yet available. For years, physician referral representatives have been asked the proverbial question, "Can you refer me to a good doctor?" They've also been asked about how often physicians perform surgery and about malpractice suits. Traditionally, hospitals have not made this information available, but, in some markets, other sources have brought it to the surface.

Consumers looking for information

Objective, credentialed physician information is available today through referral services. However, most people aren't aware that it is relatively easy to obtain. Several years ago, I was involved with a radio advertising campaign. Its main objectives were to educate the public regarding the information available about a hospital's physicians and encourage them to call for an appointment. In order to do so, simulated physician referral calls were broadcast in which information was provided regarding board certification, years in practice, medical school, residency, and additional training.

Some of you may be thinking that there was no rocket science involved in creating such commercials. I'm sure that's the opinion many had about an ad for beer bottles being washed with steam launched by the Schlitz beer company in the 1900s. The ads took Schlitz beer from fifth place to a tie for first in market share. Although I'm not suggesting a single healthcare advertising campaign is going to move the market share needle in such a drastic way, I am suggesting that there are factors in the healthcare consumerism movement that are already in place in an established hospital call center. Don't miss the opportunity to fully communicate the information in a meaningful and relevant way. Also, do not underestimate the relevancy to the consumer.

In a 2007 survey by consulting firm Booz Allen Hamilton, one of the criteria identified by consumers of high-deductible or consumer-directed health plans as most useful in determining healthcare quality was the number of years physicians had been practicing in their fields. Of the survey respondents, 89% said the information was extremely useful, very useful, or useful.[1]

Some would argue that this is too simplistic, and I would not disagree. It is not the answer to the quality question. However, coupled with other objective data—education background, board certification, honors, awards, faculty appointments, research, publications, etc.—consumers can begin to make an informed decision in their search for a physician. But today's health consumer is looking for more.

Chapter 3

In the 2007 Booz Allen survey, consumers "see doctors and hospitals competing on quality." High-deductible and consumer-directed health plan respondents were asked what quality information they would find useful. Their responses are listed in Figure 3.1.

Figure 3.1 — 2007 Booz Allen survey

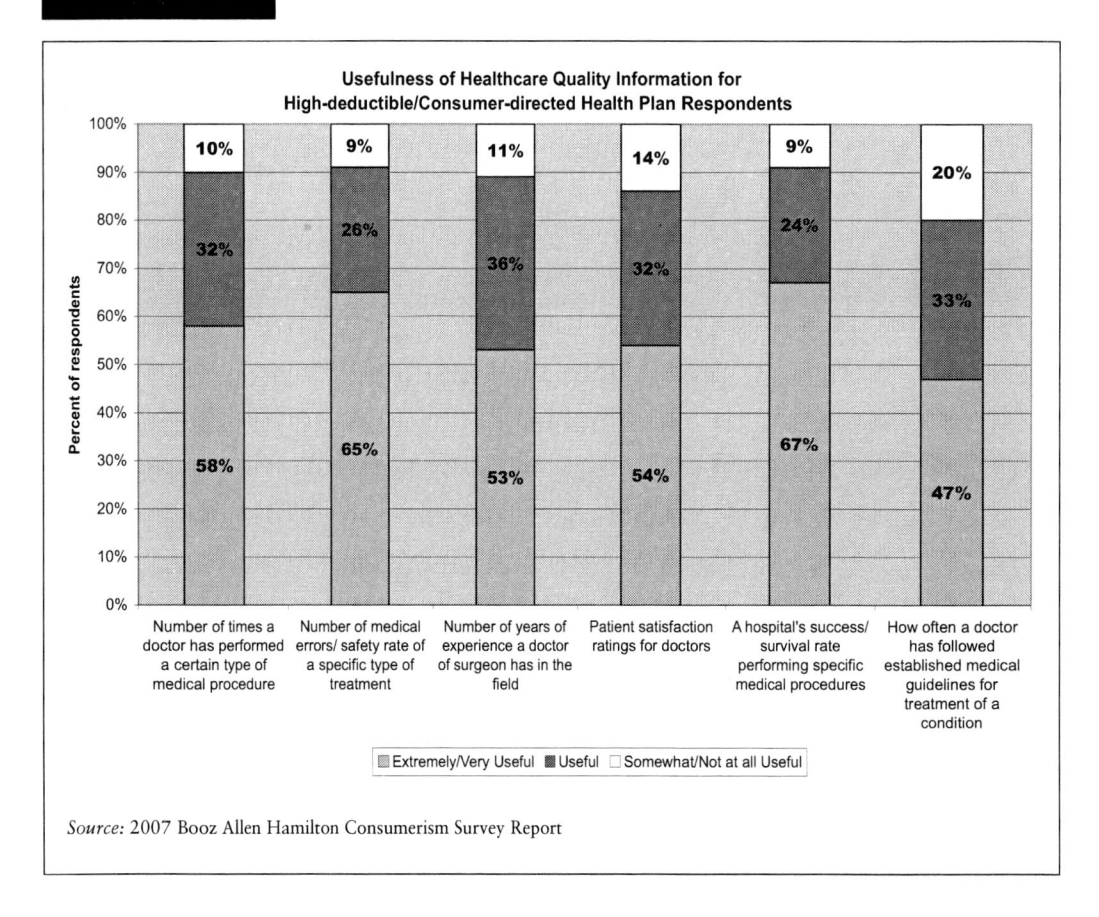

Usefulness of Healthcare Quality Information for High-deductible/Consumer-directed Health Plan Respondents

Category	Extremely/Very Useful	Useful	Somewhat/Not at all Useful
Number of times a doctor has performed a certain type of medical procedure	58%	32%	10%
Number of medical errors/safety rate of a specific type of treatment	65%	26%	9%
Number of years of experience a doctor of surgeon has in the field	53%	36%	11%
Patient satisfaction ratings for doctors	54%	32%	14%
A hospital's success/survival rate performing specific medical procedures	67%	24%	9%
How often a doctor has followed established medical guidelines for treatment of a condition	47%	33%	20%

Source: 2007 Booz Allen Hamilton Consumerism Survey Report

When asked about the value of healthcare provider cost information, 80% or more of the high-deductible and consumer-directed health plan respondents described the following information as useful or extremely useful in their decision-making process:

- Costs for specific health products or services
- Costs for entire course of care
- Average regional costs for treating a certain condition
- Individual out-of-pocket costs before a medical product or service is provided

What tends to be one of the greatest voids at this point for the consumer is the absence of information. More than 50% of those in high-deductible or consumer-directed health plans indicated dissatisfaction or only partial satisfaction with the information available regarding cost and quality. There seems to be a great deal of opportunity for any number of healthcare entities to step into the role of healthcare cost and quality information providers. There are several groups providing this information in some form today, but it is not as easily accessible as consumers have come to expect in other industries, e.g., *Consumer Reports*.

When it comes to information about the quality of a doctor and the prices charged by doctors and hospitals, consumers tend to view physicians as a more highly trusted source of this information than hospitals. Consumers trust doctors and want their help in navigating the healthcare system. For hospitals

Chapter 3

seeking to raise their credibility factor, there may be an opportunity in partnering with physicians. If consumers were to be directed by their physician to the hospital call center, seeing it as an extension of the physician's office, the hospital might be viewed as a more trusted source. In general, when talking with healthcare leaders across the country, the consensus is that the new healthcare consumer is going to be knocking at your door or, in this case, calling your phones—if not now, in the near future.

Time to start the dialogue

So what does this mean for the healthcare marketer? According to the Booz Allen survey, individuals with more financial responsibility for their healthcare are more aware of cost and quality differences. They are trying to find information so they can make decisions about products and services. However, even those in the traditional healthcare payment system have heightened awareness of cost and quality. This is due to rising premiums, deductibles, and copays, coupled with highly publicized media reports on medical errors and efforts to improve patient safety.

If your organization has not begun an internal dialogue on how to communicate cost and quality to the general public, start now.

Answering consumers' questions

AtlantiCare—introduced in Chapter 2—is already receiving questions from consumers about the quality and price of its services, says Maureen Donzuso, contact center manager at AtlantiCare. Callers contact the center with Internet information that is often inaccurate or incomplete. Although demand has not been significant to date, staff members have been trained to assist callers with cost information. They also field questions with respect to quality. Each question is individually researched, and the representative responds directly to the consumer.

At Emory Healthcare, senior executives asked the call center to name the top procedures for which callers were requesting outcome and quality data. This information was then provided back to the call center team, enabling them to communicate to callers not only the numbers, but what the components actually meant. This is consistent with the role of the call center—providing customer service and educating consumers.

Frequently requested procedures, Emory Healthcare

The following are the procedures most inquired about by consumers who call Emory Healthcare to request outcome and quality data:

Cardiothoracic surgery
Mitral valve replacement
Esophagectomy related to esophageal cancer
Off-pump coronary artery bypass surgery
Aortic aneurysm
Hyperhydrosis microinvasive
Lung volume reduction surgery

Cardiology
Arrhythmia ablation
Laser angioplasty
Plaque-shaving procedure for peripheral vascular disease

Chapter 3

General surgery
Breast reconstruction/breast cancer

Neurosurgery
Microdiscectomy
Chiari malformations

Orthopedic surgery
Kyphoplasty
Endoscopic disc surgery
Total hip replacement
Revision hip surgery
Unicondylar knee resurfacing
Total knee replacement
Total shoulder replacement

Hematology
Stem cell transplant

Ophthalmology
Cataract surgery
Lasik surgery

Transplant
Islet cell transplantation

Emory Healthcare

Ahead of the curve?

Although AtlantiCare and Emory may be ahead of their own markets with respect to demand for this information, they are already planning for the future. Both are asking questions about how to handle calls pertaining to the crucial issues of cost and quality.

Don't always try to reinvent the wheel. For example, your call center may not be best positioned to answer a question about cost. You may wonder, "If not the call center, then who?" In today's healthcare financial climate, this is often an extremely complex question. Many organizations have individuals who can serve as financial counselors. If these individuals are available at your organization, identify them and immediately let your call center team know who these people are and how they can put callers in touch with them. And remember, this is an area where a successful call transfer is critical. If a consumer is disconnected, he or she may feel dumped.

Circling back to customer service

So here we find ourselves back at service. As I said at the beginning of this chapter, the new healthcare consumers are looking for cost, quality, and service. Regardless of what payer classification one has, exceptional service is expected and should be delivered. Numerous studies show the positive effect of satisfied patients not only from a loyalty perspective, but also in the bottom line.

As I talked with call center leaders across the country, all in different markets, the universal theme from each of them was that consumers are expecting a higher level of service. They want shorter wait times, faster turn-around, greater flexibility, readily accessible information, and easy interactions. Technology has created a society accustomed to the immediate access of virtually anything via the Internet, and the slowness and inefficiencies of the healthcare system are often very frustrating to consumers.

Chapter 3

Work collaboratively with your call center leadership to talk about preparing for the new healthcare consumer. If you haven't already started asking questions about how you are going to handle consumer inquiries on cost and quality, start. Perform random, anonymous calls to your own call center, as well as those of other industries, and then benchmark your customer service against the leaders. And never take your eye off of the exceptional service target.

Cross-selling at its best

CHAPTER 4

Cross-selling at its best

Many hospital organizations are uncomfortable with the word "selling," so I recognize it is a bit risky to entitle a chapter "cross-selling," as we may lose some of you. But let's try to get past "sell" being a four-letter word and recognize that we all engage in selling in a variety of ways every day. For example, parents sell when they persuade their children to eat vegetables. Employees sell to their boss to get them to accept a proposal. Whether we actually use the word "sell" or not, the action is part of our daily lives.

When cross-selling, a sales person goes a step beyond what customers were initially inquiring about by offering them an additional product or service, thus providing customers with additional value to the interaction. The hospital marketer benefits from cross-selling by exposing a relevant audience—one that is already engaging with your organization for one product—to an additional product or service without any additional marketing expense.

Chapter 4

Within the hospital call center, the first real cross-selling initiatives began with physician referral. Call center representatives will often assist callers with finding physicians and scheduling an appointment. This is a perfect example of cross-selling. The consumer calls for a referral and the contact center representative is able to sell the additional service of a physician appointment.

Three ways to cross-sell

As hospital contact centers have become more sophisticated and more comfortable with a sales environment, organizations are using them more to cross-sell services. Generally, there are three types of cross-selling approaches deployed in today's environment.

The first of these methods is the most informal. It is simply providing call center representatives with a regularly updated list of hospital programs to be cross-sold—regardless of a caller's interests. The list changes based on when the programs are being offered and what offers have excess capacity. An example of this type of cross-selling is promoting a February heart fair to every caller during the last two weeks of January and the first week of February. In March, representatives may offer discounted memberships at the hospital fitness center. Contact center representatives are responsible for determining when they are going to cross-sell services or products, and to which callers. There is usually little or no tracking of sales with this informal approach, and representatives are not usually offered an incentive for the sell.

A second, more structured approach is one where specific programs for cross-selling have been developed. If a caller asks about a particular event or physician, or if they meet a certain demographic criteria, they would be flagged to receive information on a relevant topic. This additional information may be provided while the caller is on the phone with the representative, or it may be mailed after the fact. For example, if a consumer calls to register for a prenatal program and indicated that this is her first child, the call center representative would ask if she had selected a pediatrician, thus opening the door for a physician referral.

Another example would be callers over the age of 65 calling for flu shots. The representative can see in the database whether callers are members of the hospital's senior membership program. If not, the representative can introduce the program on the phone and then mail follow-up information about the program with a membership application.

Hospital call centers with sophisticated software systems may be aided in this type of cross-selling by pop-up screens that remind the representatives to talk with callers about these relevant programs. Such programs also tend to be tracked more closely and are aligned with the performance goals of the contact center representative.

Structured and streamlined cross-selling

The third type of cross-selling is exemplified by Community Health Network of Indianapolis. The organization has a highly structured, streamlined, and integrated cross-selling program. In collaboration with its customer relationship management (CRM) partners, CPM Marketing Group and The Beryl Companies, Debbie Kenemer, director of interactive marketing for Community, says her organization wanted to be able to proactively cross-sell to consumers calling into its contact center. One of its goals was to leverage the power of its enterprisewide database, which housed not only customer interactions, but information about noncustomers in its market. Given the extensive amount of data housed in the CRM database, the cross-sell messaging opportunities are virtually limitless. Messages to current customers could be triggered from past hospital experience (i.e., hospitals can offer support service to former patients or personalized marketing messages to potential patients based on demographic information, including a unique predictive modeling feature of their CRM database) Community is able to take advantage of CPM's proprietary predictive modeling of consumer healthcare utilization scoring to further enhance the cross-selling relevancy. The CPM predictive modeling technology is embedded into the CRM database, enabling an effective way to find at-risk prospects and patients. By passing this data along with the cross-sell script to the call center representative, a message can be prepared to create awareness of a service for the customer.

Cross-selling at its best

About Community Health Network

Indianapolis-based Community Health Network has five hospitals and more than 70 sites of care. The organization has 867 staffed beds and more than 10,000 employees.

www.ecommunity.com

When a caller to Community reaches its Beryl contact center, the data collected from the call center representative searches the health system's CRM database for the individual and almost instantly returns relevant cross-sell information to the representative. Because this is an integrated automated system, it can be programmed with "red-flag protections." For example, repeat callers do not receive the same offers as they did during a previous call.

Community has been deploying this cross-selling technique for several years, and, although every caller is a potential cross-sell candidate, there are several groups who are identified for focused efforts. One of these groups is new movers. Community knows that, most of the time, when new movers call, they are seeking a physician referral. The CRM database is able to tell the call center representative whether the caller has children living in the house. If a call comes from a household with children, a cross-sell trigger is generated for the call center representative. Beryl has worked with Community to develop a scripted cross-sell message about its pediatricians, thus providing the caller with a more valuable experience.

In late 2007, Community expanded its cross-selling initiative into a highly competitive geographic market. If a caller from its northeast region contacts the call center, the database identifies the caller as living in the region, and, depending on what the caller is requesting, a cross-selling opportunity is triggered. For example, if the caller is registering for a local event, the CRM database is searched and a script is provided for the representative to market Community's facilities and physicians.

The cross-selling messages in this system are very dynamic and constantly changing. Kenemer says the goals of the cross-selling initiative have definitely been met. "We wanted to combine our very robust CRM database and robust call center service to make the call more valuable to the caller and to the network," she says.

The approach Community has taken allows the organization to make the most out of every customer interaction. In addition, because Community's contact center data are integrated into its CRM database, the health system can track downstream interactions with the organization. More than 39,000 visits to Community and its network providers were scheduled during the past two years as a direct result of various cross-selling efforts, Kenemer says.

It's not all good

It is worthwhile to note that not all cross-selling is good. A poor cross-sell occurs when irrelevant messages are delivered to the wrong audience at the wrong time or with the wrong frequency. It is extremely important to watch for these pitfalls, or your best intentions to educate and provide a service to your customers may come across as hard sell—something that most people don't appreciate.

Cross-selling at its best

Other things to remember:

- Watch out for repeat callers and make sure they are not getting hit with the same cross-sell message every time they call.
- Make sure cross-selling isn't "one size fits all." In healthcare, there is rarely one solution for everyone.
- Allow representatives to use discretion. For example, if a caller is obviously stressed or in a crisis state, it may not be the right time for cross-selling.
- Track the results of your representatives' cross-selling efforts to assess whether it is working. If it doesn't seem to be working, Kenemer suggests reviewing the offer and the scripting. Either one could be causing the consumer to decline the offer.

If done well, cross-selling makes a call more interesting and engaging for representatives and callers. It conveys that callers were thought about beyond the immediate "transaction." For example, consider a woman who calls to inquire about a cardiac screening. The representative not only efficiently handles the request, but offers to send her the organization's *Heart Healthy Cookbook* and mentions an upcoming lecture series on women's heart disease. This conveys to the caller that someone listened and cared enough to tell her about items and events that are personally relevant.

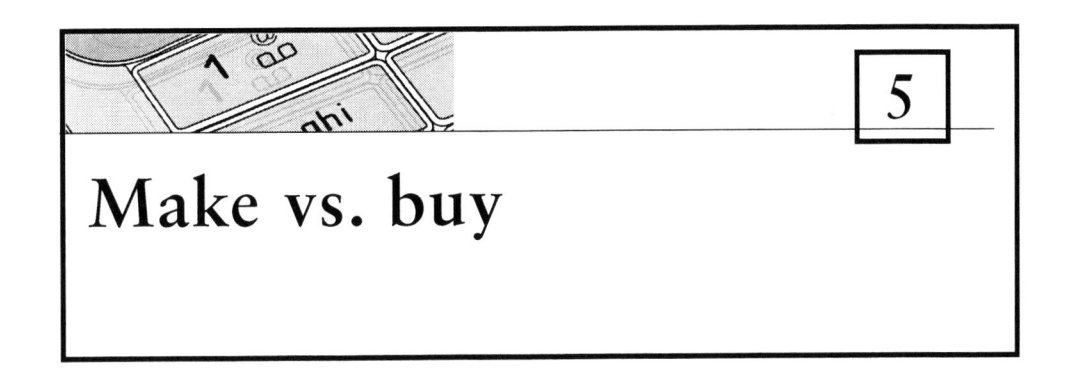

Make vs. buy

Chapter 5

Make vs. buy

Although I've implied it throughout this book thus far, I may not have explicitly stated it: The call center needs to be viewed as a vital component of an organization's operation. The call center is the virtual front door to your organization. The value placed on creating this first impression, solidifying relationships with customers, and reaching beyond the walls of the hospital are key factors to deciding on the right call center format for your hospital. You can start an in-house call center or hire an outside vendor to run the call center for you.

Although it is a significant investment, a call center needs to be viewed as a revenue center. It is a place where marketing efforts culminate, and it enables customers to begin and/or further solidify relationships with your organization. Once an organization begins to realize the value a high-functioning call center can provide, it can start to objectively explore building the center internally versus outsourcing to a third party.

CHAPTER 5

Analyze your situation

Hospitals or healthcare systems that are facing the "make vs. buy" decision are often in one of the following situations:

- They are looking to start a call center
- Their current call center is in a transitional state, such as:
  - Technology challenges
  - Increasing or decreasing call volume
  - Expanding hours of operation
  - Improving operational proficiency
- They are facing organizational challenges, such as a merger or acquisition

Richard D. Stier is a vice president at HealthLine Systems, Inc., a healthcare software and consulting firm based in San Diego. Stier recommends asking five critical questions before going into a make vs. buy decision:

1. What is the purpose of your contact center?
2. Do you want to provide transactions or transformations?
3. Are you providing a commodity or an experience?
4. Is your contact center a cost center or a revenue center?
5. What's the bottom line?

Determine its purpose

The organization needs to decide why the contact center has been or is being developed. Is it to provide physician referrals, class registrations, or general services information? Or is it to provide a centralized access point that can provide the previously mentioned services in addition to services such as physician office appointment scheduling, outpatient preregistration and scheduling, or after-hours triage? Or perhaps the primary use is to ensure that consumers have an excellent first impression of the organization.

Whether one of these reasons is yours or not, it is critical that you are clear about why your call center exists in order to determine whether an in-house or outsourced call center is best for your organization.

What will your call center provide?

The second and third questions that Stier recommends relate to the consumer's call center experience. Do you want your call center to provide transactions or transformations? Transactions can be easily outsourced, but transformations are much more difficult, because they go beyond the generic providing of information. They establish a personal connection with a caller or a memorable moment that will form a lasting relationship.

Similarly, do you want your call center to provide a commodity or an experience? Many physician referral services are commodities with the same call

Chapter 5

flow and same type of information presented to each caller. However, some have moved past mere commodity to enhance the call with personalized service that creates a memorable experience for the caller. For example, talking with the consumer about relevant hospital classes, events, and services that are related to the reason for the physician referral call (or cross-selling as discussed in Chapter 4) make the call more personalized, leaving a longer-lasting positive impression.

Cost vs. revenue

Next, Stier asks you to consider whether your contact center is a cost center or a revenue center. Depending on the call volume, it may be more cost-effective for some organizations to outsource than to maintain an in-house call center. However, the more important question is about outsourcing a revenue-generating department. If your organization has determined that the call center is a revenue center and not a cost center, then is outsourcing the best choice? "Would your hospital outsource its open heart surgery program?" asks Stier.

Paul Spiegelman, founder and CEO of The Beryl Companies, says he feels a call center should be looked at as a profit center, not as a cost center. Beryl, headquartered in Bedford, TX, is a provider of outsourced telephone and Web-based communications for healthcare organizations.

Each call represents $4,000 in downstream revenue, so there is ample evidence to either invest in call center infrastructure or consider outsourcing.[2] With most hospitals struggling to achieve or maintain a positive margin, this revenue can be the difference between losing money and making a profit. Because hospital call centers are often under-resourced, a switch to an outsourced partner operating 24/7 may be worthwhile, although not necessarily a less-expensive option. However, according to Spiegelman, "the ROI in having a well-run call center is so significant that the additional cost becomes immaterial."

The bottom line

The fifth question Stier suggests considering is the contact center's ROI. He recommends that an organization should examine the call center's projected ROI for three years to decide whether to make or buy. In some cases, owning an in-house contact center can provide a greater ROI in subsequent years.

A true comparison

To get a sense of the costs involved in the call center operation, an objective comparison between an in-house operation and one that is outsourced is vital. But such a comparison is often difficult to obtain.

To help hospitals understand the direct and indirect expenses associated with a call center operation, Beryl has developed a tool that compares costs between an in-house call center, an expanded 24/7 in-house call center, and an outsourced 24/7 call center. Figure 5.1 can be used to help an organization complete an analysis that identifies the real costs associated with each option.

Chapter 5

Figure 5.1 Hospital Call Center Build vs. Buy Analysis Tool

Costs associated with operating a hospital/health system call center	Hospital/system internal call center (current)	hospital/system internal call center (expand to 24/7)	Outsource with 24/7 access
Gather basic assumption information:			
Monthly calls handled (average monthly volume)			
Monthly letter volume (% of calls that generate a letter)			
Monthly telecom minutes			
Number of call advisors or customer service reps			
Number of supervisors (if applicable)			
Number of managers (if applicable)			
Number of Web support and IT support staff			
Calculate call center set-up/ capital requirements:			
Quality monitoring (servers, software, annual support and training)			
Equipment (switch, hardware, licenses, installation, programming, maintenance, T1 phone lines)			
Workstations (furniture, equipment, PC, phone, headset, printer)			
Staff training (new software and protocols, time away from training)			
Recruitment costs			
Total call center setup/ cash requirement:	A		
Call center operations expenses			
Direct costs			
Call advisors/customer service reps (salary and benefits)			
Call advisor/multilingual (salary and benefits)			

54   Turn Calls into Customers

Make vs. buy

Figure 5.1 Hospital Call Center Build vs. Buy Analysis Tool (cont.)

Costs associated with operating a hospital/health system call center	Hospital/system internal call center (current)	hospital/system internal call center (expand to 24/7)	Outsource with 24/7 access
Supervisors (salary and benefits, if applicable)			
Managers (salary and benefits, if applicable)			
IT support (salary and benefits)			
Annual software license			
Telecom (line charges + usage)			
Supplies (office supplies, letterhead, envelopes, promotional items, brochures, business cards)			
Fulfillment (postage and handling)			
Total direct costs	B		
Indirect costs:			
Rent/building			
Utilities			
Real estate taxes			
Internal IT, accounting, HR, facilities support			
Insurance			
Workers' compensation			
Professional liability			
Commercial and excess liability			
Total indirect costs	C		
Total call center operations expenses (B + C)	B		
TOTAL COSTS (A + D)			
Divide total costs by projected call volume to determine total projected cost per call			

Source: The Beryl Companies

Turn Calls into Customers   55

Chapter 5

But there's another point of consideration in evaluating the true value a call center can deliver. Consumer-driven health is forcing healthcare executives to view their organizations as a more traditional retail business. Price, quality, and customer service have become important factors for success as more consumers take charge of their health-spending decisions. The benefits of positive long-term relationships translate into goodwill, which in turn translates into revenue.

Spiegelman says most hospitals use their call center for the more traditional services, such as physician referral and class/event registration. To build lasting relationships with consumers, hospitals must engage them at every point in the healthcare delivery process. Call centers can play a valuable role in that process while contributing to an organization's overall profitability.

If you outsource

If your call center is going to be outsourced, Beryl suggests the following 10 tips to ensure success:

- Engage in a true partnership; require commitment by the hospital and the call center provider. Everyone has to be prepared to assign the appropriate resources to make the relationship successful.
- Select a partner that understands the healthcare industry, hospital operations, and healthcare delivery.
- Use the data gathered during call interactions to show an ROI for your hospital's marketing efforts.

- Use available technology to minimize the implications of call volume fluctuations.
- Commit to ongoing training for call center representatives that includes customer service, healthcare terminology, and the hospitals they will represent. This training should equip them with everything they need to have an authentic engagement with customers, including voice, tone, and empathy.
- Understand the various levels of support your call center partner will provide. Who will handle operations issues? Who will handle strategic issues? How can the call center provider align its strategies with your strategic plans?
- Develop an annual action plan with accountabilities and measurements.
- Don't underestimate the value of experience.
- How will the call center provider assist you in using call center data to build customer relationship management capabilities?
- Select a partner that is able to grow to meet changing hospital needs.

Due to the significant investment involved, the decision to make vs. buy should be made after a great deal of thought and consideration of your organization's strategic direction. Either option can be successfully executed if an organization realizes that its contact center is a vital, strategic component of its operation.

Demonstrating credible ROI to the C-suite

6

CHAPTER 6

Demonstrating credible ROI to the C-suite

Depending on who you are talking to about the topic of return on investment (ROI), you may get an assortment of answers about what marketing ROI is. Some people will talk about ROI in terms of market share. Someone else may respond with "revenue reconciliation." Others will converse about call volume, cost per call, and appointment conversion rates. Still others may consider all of these to be ROI measurements. However, the goal of this chapter isn't simply to provide a laundry list of possible metrics that the marketer can use. Instead, the goal is to take one step back and establish which ROI metrics are going to be credible to your organization's senior leadership.

To determine credible ROI reporting, there needs to be thoughtful, collaborative, and integrated planning to establish what the strategic purpose of the contact center is. There needs to be discussion with members of senior leadership to understand their expectations for the contact center, including desired outcome measurements. I am not suggesting you go in with a blank piece of paper and ask to have this information handed to you. Marketing and call

Chapter 6

center leaders must be prepared to discuss their ideas, thoughts, and recommendations. Reaching agreement on the purpose of the contact center is critical, as it will drive not only credible ROI tracking, but future decision-making.

Four call center models

One approach to guiding the discussion on the purpose of the contact center and the subsequent ROI metrics is suggested by Richard D. Stier, vice president of HealthLine Systems, introduced in Chapter 5. In Figure 6.1, four different contact center models are suggested.

In the first model, the call center purpose is to be a community resource. Most often in this environment, the call center is providing physician referrals, class and event registrations, and general hospital/health system information. Usually, the metrics that are tracked in this call center are transaction oriented—the number of inbound calls, number of referrals made, number of class/event registrations, etc. These metrics will not suffice as credible ROI in the executive suite. They may be good barometers of what is immediately working with marketing calls to action, but they are not generally viewed as outcome-oriented ROI. Credible ROI should be thought of in terms of a financial measurement. Although call center transactions are necessary operational indicators for the call center manager and the marketer, they are not the strategic-outcome measurements a senior executive is seeking.

Figure 6.1 Contract Center Models

Expand your contact center's influence

Commitment — Degree of INFLUENCE — Compliance

Preferred Access
ExtremeService
Targeted Growth
Community Resource

Length of TIME

© Richard D. Stier for HealthLine Systems, Inc., 2008

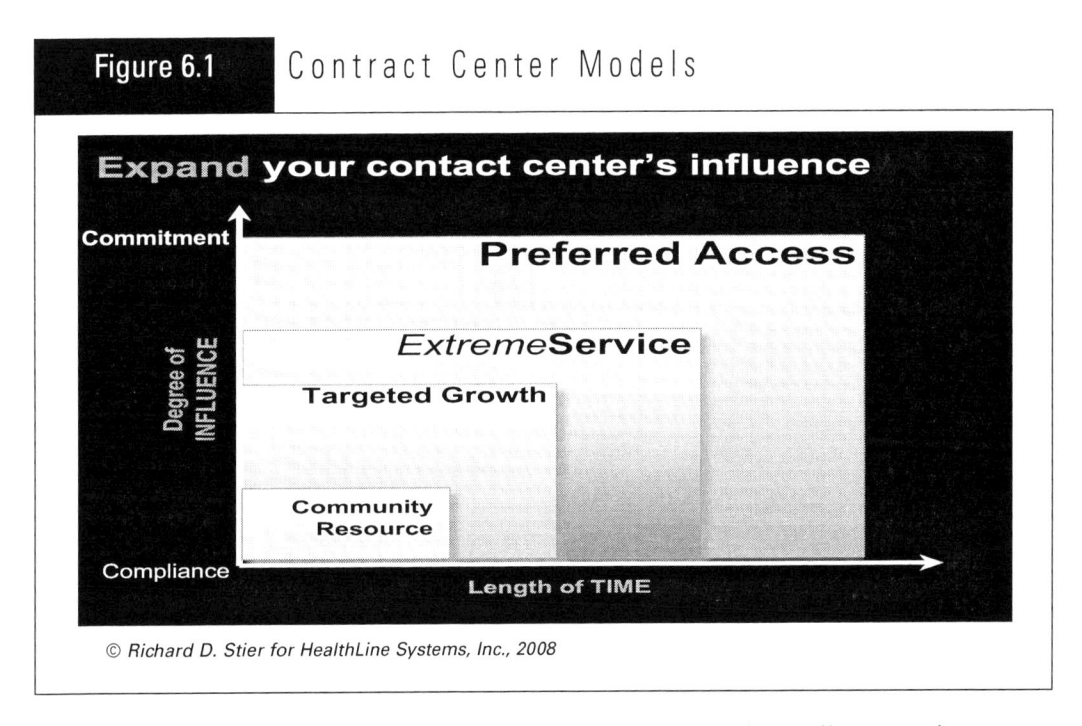

For the organization looking to expand the influence of its call center, the next opportunity would be targeted growth. In this model, the contact center wants to create incremental growth for carefully selected services. The contact center engaged in targeted growth incorporates cross-selling of high-margin services, conducts inbound and outbound calls, and focuses on customer relationship management activities. Metrics then begin to take on more traditional ROI measurements, such as net contribution, physician appointment, and cross-sell rates.

The ExtremeService contact center serves as the front door to the organization that desires to showcase extraordinary service. There is a deliberate focus on creating a memorable experience for the caller at this type of contact center. In addition to the previously mentioned metrics, there are outcome measurements of satisfaction, loyalty, repeat utilization, lifetime value, share of wallet, and share of household.

Preferred Access contact centers are the central hub for virtually all incoming and outgoing communication with an organization. They manage Web, fax, mail, voice, and e-mail correspondence with customers. These contact centers may also provide appointment scheduling, preregistration, disease management, and after-hours triage for physician offices. Additional metrics of ROI include cost savings resulting from integrated functions, dollars saved in triaging patients to the appropriate level of care, and measurable health outcomes.

Know what your organization wants

A set of common definitions within your organization is also essential for credible ROI reporting. One of the most complex aspects of revenue tracking is ensuring data reliability. This may involve working with the chief financial officer. Establishing the source of this financial data and the understanding of how the numbers are derived is critical in understanding the ROI calculations. Marketers need to work with their financial colleagues to agree upon how their organization is going to calculate marketing ROI. You must consider factors beyond reductions for contractual allowances, such as bad debt and direct, indirect, and overhead expenses.

It is also crucial to determine how downstream revenue will be attributed to individuals. For example, a customer calls the contact center after receiving a mailing for a new parent class. After attending the class, the customer becomes an orthopedic patient and uses other hospital services. Will the hospital consider the downstream revenue generated to be part of the original campaign's ROI? Or will the ROI be limited to the customer's attendance at the new parent class?

Common ROI decisions that need to be agreed upon in advance are:

- How much time needs to elapse before someone is considered a repeat patient vs. a new patient?
- Are repeat/retained patients going to be included in the ROI calculation?
- How are you going to answer the question, "Wouldn't the patient still have come to us anyway?" Are control groups going to be used or is market share going to be factored out?
- How much time will be allowed between initial marketing and downstream utilization? One year? Two years? Or will it vary by service line?
- How frequently is ROI reporting going to be done?

For marketers who are new to ROI reporting, the book *A Marketer's Guide to Measuring ROI: Tools to Track the Returns from Healthcare Marketing Efforts,* by David Marlowe, provides a step-by-step guide to getting started with this significant endeavor. ROI tracking and reporting is challenging, especially depending on what infrastructure resources your organization has.

Chapter 6

Reporting of ROI to senior executives can often be cumbersome and may fail to clearly demonstrate how the reporting ties to the strategic goals of an organization. Using a report-card format, HealthLine Systems, Inc., has prepared a series of figures that demonstrates how an ROI report can provide an overview for the senior executive. Figure 6.2 shows how a call center's activity has supported two of its organization's strategic goals and also identifies future opportunities for improvement.

Figure 6.2 Sample ROI Report Card

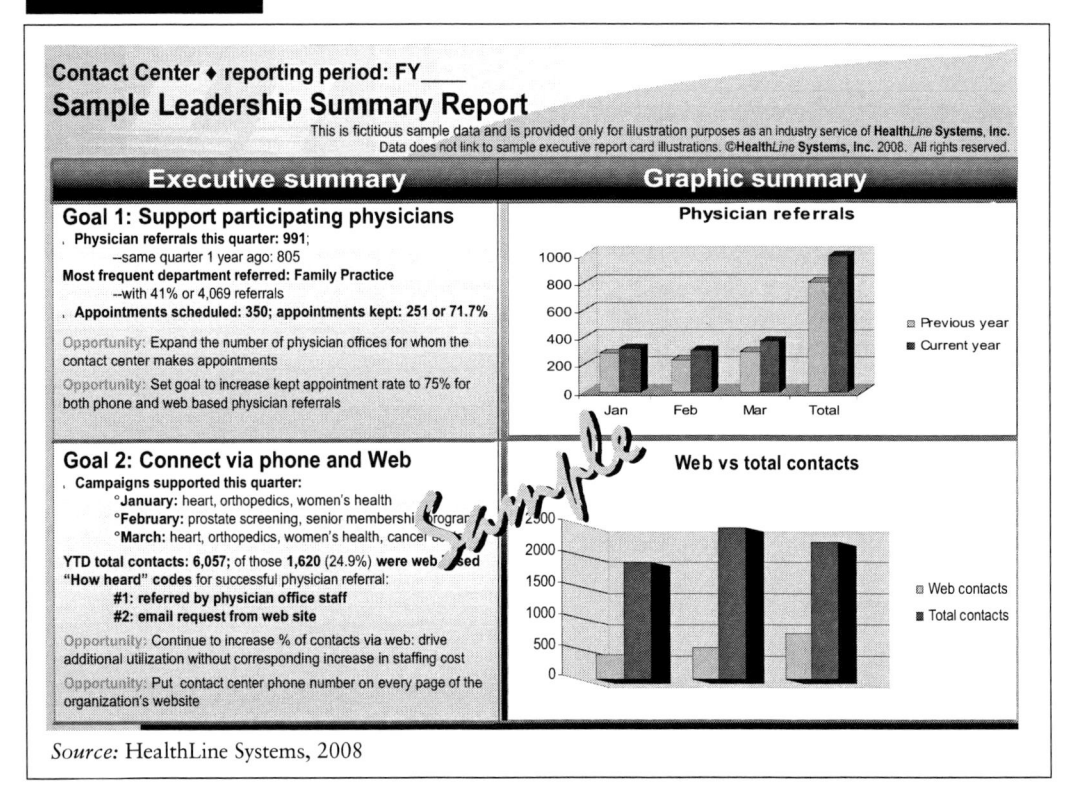

Contact Center ♦ reporting period: FY____
Sample Leadership Summary Report

This is fictitious sample data and is provided only for illustration purposes as an industry service of HealthLine Systems, Inc. Data does not link to sample executive report card illustrations. ©HealthLine Systems, Inc. 2008. All rights reserved.

Executive summary	Graphic summary

Goal 1: Support participating physicians
• Physician referrals this quarter: 991;
  --same quarter 1 year ago: 805
Most frequent department referred: Family Practice
  --with 41% or 4,069 referrals
• Appointments scheduled: 350; appointments kept: 251 or 71.7%
Opportunity: Expand the number of physician offices for whom the contact center makes appointments
Opportunity: Set goal to increase kept appointment rate to 75% for both phone and web based physician referrals
	Physician referrals (bar chart: Jan, Feb, Mar, Total; Previous year vs Current year)

Goal 2: Connect via phone and Web
• Campaigns supported this quarter:
  °**January:** heart, orthopedics, women's health
  °**February:** prostate screening, senior membership program
  °**March:** heart, orthopedics, women's health, cancer
YTD total contacts: 6,057; of those 1,620 (24.9%) were web based
"How heard" codes for successful physician referral:
  #1: referred by physician office staff
  #2: email request from web site
Opportunity: Continue to increase % of contacts via web: drive additional utilization without corresponding increase in staffing cost
Opportunity: Put contact center phone number on every page of the organization's website
	Web vs total contacts (bar chart; Web contacts vs Total contacts)

Source: HealthLine Systems, 2008

Demonstrating credible ROI to the C-suite

In Figure 6.3, the call center activity is translated into visits and downstream revenue: emergency department, outpatient visits, inpatient admissions, and physician office appointments scheduled by the call center. It ties to strategic alignment by highlighting priority service lines for the organization.

Figure 6.3 Sample Executive Report Card, Page 1

Contact Center ♦ reporting period: FY____
Sample Executive Report Card page 1

This is fictitious sample data and is provided only for illustration purposes as an industry service of HealthLine Systems, Inc.
©HealthLine Systems, Inc. 2008. All rights reserved.

Executive Briefing Note: All inpatient admissions and outpatient visits subsequent to interaction with contact center	Priority Service Line Measures	Contact Center Operations Indicators
Estimated net contribution: $1,018,958 **ROI per $1 invested:** $3.05 **Incremental gross revenue:** $4,680,200 **Inpatient admissions:** 311 **Outpatient visits:** 1,980 **ER cases:** 414	**Heart Center** Inpatient admissions: 6 Outpatient visits: 28 **Cancer Center** Inpatient admissions: 8 Outpatient visits: 32 **Orthopedic** Inpatient admissions: 14 Outpatient visits: 75	**Total contacts:** 16,500 Phone: 15,000 Web: 1,500 **Total physician referrals:** 4,890 **Appointments scheduled:** 1,467 (30%) **Kept appointment rate:** 72% **Abandonment rate:** 8% **Average seconds to service:** 39 **Priorities for improvement:** 1: ____ 2: ____ 3: ____

Source: HealthLine Systems, 2008

Figures 6.4 and 6.5 provide a quick reference of the established ROI formula. These straightforward illustrations of financial calculations can help stifle what I call "marketing ROI skepticism," which sometimes happens even after an agreement has been reached on ROI calculation methods.

CHAPTER 6

Figure 6.4 Sample Executive Report Card, Page 2

Your Contact Center ♦ reporting period: FY____
Sample Executive Report Card page 2

This is fictitious sample data and is provided only for illustration purposes as an industry service of HealthLine Systems, Inc.
HealthLine Systems, Inc. 2008. All rights reserved.

Contact Center Volume	
Current number of phone contacts	15,000
Current number of incremental Web/e-mail contacts	1,500
Total phone and web contacts	**16,500**
Matched Gross Revenue	
Resulting inpatient admissions matched from **Sharp Focus** – 311 (Results in average $ per inpatient admission of $11,000)	$3,421,000
Resulting outpatient visits matched from **Sharp Focus** – 1,980 (Results in average $ per outpatient visit of $500)	990,000
Resulting ER cases matched from **Sharp Focus** – 414 (Results in average $ per ER visit of just over $650)	269,200
Documented Gross Revenue	**$4,680,200**

Figure 6.5 Sample Executive Report Card, Page 3

Your Contact Center ♦ reporting period: FY____
Sample Executive Report Card page 3

This is fictitious sample data and is provided only for illustration purposes as an industry service of HealthLine Systems, Inc.
HealthLine Systems, Inc. 2008. All rights reserved.

Estimated Net Contribution	
Documented gross revenue from **Sharp Focus**	$4,680,200
Less market share ("business that would have come here anyway") (10%)	(468,020)
Total gross revenue less market share	4,212,180
Less managed care discounts and bad debt (50%)	(2,106,090)
Net gross revenue before operating cost	2,106,090
Less variable cost per case or discharge (@ 35%) (variable cost of care)	(737,132)
Less contact center direct operating cost	(350,000)
Estimated Net Contribution from contact center (A)	**$1,018,958**
Estimated ROI	
Contact center direct operating cost **(B)**	($350,000)
Direct revenue from contracts for services **(C)**	$50,000
Net Operating Cost of contact center	($300,000)
Return on Investment per $1 invested (A+C)/B Industry standard 3:1 based on study of over 800,000 calls over four years	**$3.05**

Source: HealthLine Systems, 2008

Most call center software systems have a component that helps facilitate this ROI process. There are also outsourced solutions in which hospital data can be sent to a third party for matching and report generation. Other organizations have pursued enterprisewide CRM database systems, which pull contact center, direct marketing, hospital utilization, and financial data together into a single database to allow an organization to track and report information at very detailed levels.

Tracking ROI: A necessary step

Regardless of which ROI tracking method your hospital chooses, the contact center should be responsible for the tracking. Due to the resource commitment required and the fact that people often stop requesting the information, many call centers abandon ROI tracking. This is unwise. Make a point of regularly meeting with your senior leadership to review results, strategic alignment, and future goals for the call center. Consider it an investment in your future viability and growth.

7

CRM comes to healthcare: Stories from other industries

CHAPTER 7

CRM comes to healthcare: Stories from other industries

In summer 2007, there was a rip in the right shoe of my favorite pair of casual shoes. I had ordered them only five months earlier from Lands' End, so I called to order a replacement pair and was greeted by a friendly call center representative. As I began the order, the representative said she noticed I had placed this exact order five months earlier. After I explained the situation, she said that I should simply return the shoes and the company would send me new ones. I began to tell her that I had worn the shoes and the rip was probably my fault, but she assured me that the shoes should not have ripped in five months and a new pair would be shipped to me. She asked me how I would prefer to return the shoes—through the mail or at a store. Since errands were on my agenda, I opted for the store.

I suspected that the service experience might break down once I got to the store, but not so. I walked in with my obviously well-worn pair of shoes and the associate brought up my information seamlessly. The old shoes were quickly on their way back to Lands' End. Two days later, new shoes were at

Chapter 7

my front door. Lands' End had shipped the replacement shoes before the old ones had even gotten back to the warehouse.

Does Lands' End have a loyal customer? You bet. This is the second time I've had this type of exceptional service experience with this company. Although Lands' End cannot be my sole retailer, they are the first place I go for products within its category.

What made this an exceptional experience? Largely, it was the company's knowledge of me as a customer at multiple access points, and the willingness to provide an unexpected solution to a problem with its product. By taking back a product that had not lived up to the company's standards, Lands' End created a positive and memorable customer experience. I interacted with the company's Web site, call center, and store. After the initial interaction, I didn't have to repeat all of my information to anyone again. The opportunity for creating the positive experience developed simply because the call center representative recognized that I had done previous business with Lands' End. The store associate closed the deal by efficiently and effectively handling the business transaction.

Was this excellent service a matter of luck? I don't believe so. Lands' End has a long history of being committed to the customer relationship. It was one of the first retailers to embrace the Internet, and it wanted a customer's Internet experience to build upon the expertise of the contact center representatives. The company also recognized the benefit early on of working toward a connected, integrated system so that regardless of where the customer interacted with the organization, the experience was seamless. The Lands' End Web site states: "Lands' End operates on the principle that what is best for the customer is also best for the company."[3]

CRM: Part of a bigger strategy

CRM has different definitions depending on who you talk with, even among leading experts in the field. Generally, the CRM process starts with an understanding of your customers and their expectations on an individual level. It is then up to an organization to align its business objectives and processes to build customer loyalty and profitable growth over time. In its simplest terms, CRM is about understanding what is important to your customers and what is important to your organization. Hundreds of millions of dollars—some experts speculate billions—have been spent in failed CRM launches, and it is estimated that more than half of all CRM initiatives don't yield positive results. Healthcare organizations cannot afford these failed attempts and can learn much from other industries.

CRM needs to be embedded in a broader, two-fold organizational strategy. First, what is the organization's customer strategy? Many hospitals and health systems have pursued service-excellence strategies, but that is only part of a customer strategy. It involves identification and segmentation of all customer groups, leading to acquisition and retention strategies and marketing goals for each customer segment.

Chapter 7

This is a complex plan to develop, but the second part of the organizational strategy is perhaps even more difficult to complete—creating a culture that embraces the customer strategy and the CRM philosophy. As simple as my encounter with Lands' End may have seemed, had the sales associate not known what to do with the shoes, or—worse yet—refused to handle the return, my experience would have been very different. Throughout the entire organization, there is a culture that embraces the customer strategy of Lands' End.

Not just software

A common mistake is thinking that CRM is a technology deployment or a software system. Given the need to have a vast amount of data be relevant, readily available, and customizable for an audience of one, some people have a tendency to believe technology is the immediate solution. But the key to success is good strategy. Technology is simply a tool to help fulfill marketing goals.

Customer experience management

CRM is already evolving from relationship management to experience management. Organizations must focus on creating positive experiences for customers. During the past 20 years, Harley Davidson has focused on creating relationships and positive experiences for its customers. Faced with numerous challenges and near bankruptcy, this organization reinvented not only its product and processes, but its way of interacting with customers. Harley Davidson learned that it needed to build real, two-way relationships with potential and existing customers.

Harley Davidson has translated this philosophy into tangible experiences with its customers. For example, nearly every weekend, company executives participate in motorcycle events across the country to provide direct interaction with customers. This helps them gather information that can be stored in a database and used to track customer requests. The Harley Owners Group (HOG®) is a loyalty program that now has 1 million members. This group creates a family feel for Harley owners, offering events, special benefits, newsletters, and local chapters. HOG even has its own call center, where it is not unusual to have customer interactions that last as long as four hours. Unlike many contact centers, the goal is not to reduce talk time, but to bond with the customer, build a relationship, and further enhance the experience of owning a Harley. There is even an "Experience" section on its Web site that features upcoming motorcycle events, information on how to rent a Harley, on-site factory tours, trip planning tools, and an assortment of other "experiential" features.[4] For the motorcycle enthusiast, the Web site strives to create a memorable experience.

It's okay to start small

CRM requires aligning your business objectives with what customers want. Customers want personalization, relevancy, timeliness, consistency, and recognition of past interactions. Starting with the customer and focusing on creating positive experiences is the key. Formulating a customer strategy—including CRM—is an enormous undertaking. But you don't have to wait until you get it all figured out to start.

Chapter 7

If your organization knows something works already for one area, take it and run with it. You don't need to reinvent the wheel. For example, one travel organization started its CRM initiative by expanding an existing manager's thank-you note program. This manager would send thank-you notes to clients who had recently purchased travel services. The company found that customers liked this and it was a good way of getting additional feedback about the business. Because of its success, the program was expanded companywide, and the rest of the managers were directed to send notes to their clients, too. It was simple and easy to execute. Think big, but know that it's all right to start small.

Case studies and best practices in clinical services integration

CHAPTER 8

Case studies and best practices in clinical services integration

Although many hospitals have recognized that call centers are a powerful marketing tool, others have realized the call center offers another opportunity—integration with clinical services. I have had the opportunity to build these programs into a traditional marketing call center and have found them to be beneficial for clinicians and patients. Most clinicians have limited office time and find it difficult to successfully complete telephone calls, which can be particularly time-consuming. It is not uncommon for them to experience telephone-tag with their patients. Calling patients back often gets moved to the bottom of the things-to-do list, with patient visits getting more immediate attention.

Some of these calls, both to and from patients, are ideally suited for the call center to manage, as they enable consumers to immediately speak to a representative who is able to assist them. This immediate availability of information and triaging can improve health outcomes and reduce costs. However, traditional marketing call centers have not historically been involved with improving health outcomes or reducing healthcare costs.

Chapter 8

Clinical services cannot be incorporated into an existing operation without careful planning and senior leadership endorsement. It will affect how a marketer measures return on investment (ROI). Visits to the hospital may decline with a particular patient population, as you will see in one of the following case studies. This is generally not aligned with a marketing ROI measurement. However, when a hospital is engaged with the telephonic management of healthcare, declining visits may very well be a desired outcome.

The skill set of call center representatives may need to change as a call center migrates toward clinical services integration. Sometimes, this will mean the addition of registered nurses or other clinical staff members to the team, if they weren't already part of it. The clinical nature of the types of calls and the organizational culture will often determine the time for introducing nurses into the call center. Even if the call types do not change enough to require a licensed professional, the level of training changes the skill set of representatives handling the calls. These calls are generally less transactional, requiring representatives to think on their feet and know when to escalate the call to a different level.

At one call center I was involved with, calls were made to patients of the hospital emergency department 24–48 hours after the visit in order to measure patients' satisfaction levels. Other than ensuring that the patients had scheduled follow-up appointments with their physicians, there were no clinical components to these calls—they were purely to assess satisfaction. Nonclinical staff members were trained to understand the cues and scenarios that required calls to be escalated to a member of the nursing call center staff. This process required judgment and good listening skills, as the nonclinical staff would identify patients who might need clinical triaging from a nurse.

One of these calls led to the identification of a patient who needed to see the doctor immediately instead of waiting the two weeks until his next scheduled appointment. Later that day, the patient was in the operating room undergoing open heart surgery. Clinical programs integrated with contact centers can—and do—have a positive effect on the patients.

Managing children's asthma care

Robert Strunk, MD, a pulmonologist at St. Louis Children's Hospital (SLCH), a member of BJC HealthCare, and a national leader in pediatric asthma care, approached Julie Bruns, the organization's director of the call center and market research. A long-time supporter of the contact center, Strunk had an idea for an asthma-care management program modeled after the National Institute of Health's algorithm for urgent asthma management. Jointly, they took the proposed program to the call center's physician advisory board. Strunk's persistence paid off. After some initial hesitancy, the board approved the implementation of the program in 2001. Eventually, the board understood how this initiative could make a big difference in the lives of patients and their families.

Asthma assistance a phone call away

BJC HealthCare's call center provides after-hours triage services for 215 pediatricians in its service area, sponsored by SLCH. The call center is the primary contact for parents when a physician's office is closed. The asthma care management program is a specific, intentional departure from the other triage guidelines practiced within the call center. Instead of providing assessment and then referral to the appropriate level of care, this protocol calls for treatment advice, callbacks by the nurse, and prescription of oral steroids based on standing orders from the patient's primary care provider.

This program is exceptional at many levels for SLCH. First, it allows the organization to address a great community need, as asthma is pervasive in the region. Strategically, this is an important component of the overall asthma care at SLCH and has been referenced in its various national-ranking applications. Second, this has been well received by the organization's pediatricians. Last, and most important, SLCH pursued this program because it felt it was in the best interest of the children and parents it serves.

Introducing the program to the physician community

When the program was initially introduced, information was mailed to the pediatrician subscribers outlining the new process, which included optional standing orders for albuterol and prednisone. At the initial program launch, two-thirds began participating. For those physicians who did not sign on, when their patients called with an asthma attack, the triage nurses simply

Case studies and best practices in clinical services integration

transferred the call to the on-call pediatrician. After seeing the results, many other pediatrician subscribers signed on. Currently, 97% (63 out of 65) of the pediatric practices use the asthma management protocol for their patients.

Results

The improved patient outcomes have been impressive for this initiative. Prior to this new protocol, 55% of patients required second-level intervention, either in the emergency department or through consulting with an on-call physician. Now, with the new protocol, only 42% of patients required second-level intervention.

BJC plans to measure other indicators, such as reductions in school absenteeism and the number of days parents take off from work. As mentioned previously, these are not your usual marketing ROI measurements. Did SLCH decrease the admissions to its emergency department by implementing this program? Yes. Did it increase its cost per call? Yes, as it takes longer to handle these multistep calls. Yet the goals of this program are clearly being met. SLCH was not intending to achieve a financial ROI on this program; its goal was "to do what's right for kids," as its mission states. Bruns says she has "unwavering support from administration on this program because it's in the best interest of the child."

Cleveland Clinic

Cleveland Clinic made the decision to integrate disease management into its call center. Disease management services are provided for four patient populations: patients with seizure disorders (adult and pediatric), asthma, and congestive

Chapter 8

heart failure. A specific protocol for use with each patient population was either created from scratch or revised from its standard nursing triage protocols. When the physician's office closes, the phones are forwarded to the call center, where the patient's call is triaged.

What is particularly unique about Cleveland Clinic's disease management programs is the ability for the call center nurses to access the organization's electronic medical record (EMR) system. Nurses can see what kind of treatment or conditions the patients had at their last doctor visit, any new medications ordered, new treatment regimes, or changes in patient instructions provided by the physician. In addition, call center nurses document the triage details and the outcome of the call into the EMR, enabling the physician and/or advance practice nurse (APN) to make a note of the after-hours contact. Although call center nurses can still page the physician and/or APN, the ability to view and document directly into the EMR provides valuable insight, resulting in an entirely new level of quality and continuity of care.

Case studies and best practices in clinical services integration

About Cleveland Clinic

Cleveland Clinic is a nonprofit, multispecialty, academic medical center that integrates clinical and hospital care with research and education. In addition to its Cleveland location, the organization has 14 family health and ambulatory surgery centers in surrounding communities and an extensive system of community hospitals. It also operates Cleveland Clinic Florida and the Cleveland Clinic Canada Health and Wellness Center, Toronto. With 1,600 physicians representing 120 specialties and subspecialties, Cleveland Clinic annually serves 2.8 million outpatients and nearly 70,000 hospital admissions.

Its call center handles more than 1 million calls annually. In addition to disease management, the call center provides:

- Nurse triage
- Health information
- Physician referral
- Outpatient appointment registration and scheduling
- Physician office appointment scheduling
- Physician-to-physician consult
- Class registration

www.clevelandclinic.com

Clinical research at the call center

Clinical research is another area that is particularly well-suited for integration into the hospital call center. Two organizations featured in this chapter—Sharp HealthCare and Emory Healthcare—are engaged in telephonic clinical research trials in different capacities.

Chapter 8

> **About Sharp HealthCare**
>
> Sharp HealthCare is a nonprofit, integrated, regional healthcare delivery system based in San Diego. Sharp's system has 1,648 licensed beds at four acute care hospitals and three specialty hospitals, three medical groups, plus a full spectrum of other facilities and services. Sharp was named a recipient of the 2007 Malcolm Baldrige National Quality Award.
>
> *www.sharp.com*

The Sharp contact center provides physician referral, class and event registration, and general organization information. Nurse representatives provide triage for affiliated physicians from two medical groups and the Sharp Health Plan. In addition to the clinical research study, another unique service provided by the call center is mystery shopping, which I will feature in Chapter 9. The contact center has an annual call volume of 180,000.

Because of its reputation of exceptional customer service, as well as having the necessary software and call center infrastructure, Sharp's contact center was approached by the hospital's orthopedic program to conduct outbound calls to patients who had undergone total joint (hip or knee) replacements at Sharp hospitals. This program tracks post-surgery progress by calling patients after 30 days, one year, and three, five, seven, and 10 years. During these calls, approximately 40 questions are asked to determine the progress of the patient. The results are provided to Sharp's clinical effectiveness department, which processes the research and sends the information to a national committee.

Once again, this program is not being done to achieve a traditional marketing ROI. However, it is well aligned with Sharp's strategic performance improvement initiative, "The Sharp Experience," first launched in 2001. The initiative's goals are to make the organization the best place to work, practice medicine, and receive care. Kelly Faley, director of marketing technology, says the total joint outbound call center program promotes customer service and contributes to quality data for learning and best practices.

Emory's call center prescreens

Clinical trial enrollment can be a difficult task. Coordinators of the studies are often not office-bound, and it can be difficult to field calls from interested study participants. Prescreening of study participants is a process that can be lengthy, and, if the candidate is not qualified, the coordinator can be left spending a great deal of time trying to help the person find other resources. At any given time, Emory Healthcare's call center is fielding calls for a variety of clinical trials. The call center works with the clinical trial coordinators to define prescreening requirements for each clinical trial. If callers aren't eligible, they are asked whether they would like to be contacted about participating in future trials that they may be eligible for. The call center registered nurses search various databases to find other clinical trials that may be suitable for a particular caller. If nothing matches, they create a record of the caller's interest in future trial participation. This initiative strategically supports Emory's research efforts and supports its office of clinical trials, and, indirectly, its physicians.

CHAPTER 8

AtlantiCare

The last example of an organization that has chosen to integrate its contact center with clinical services is AtlantiCare, introduced in Chapter 2. AtlantiCare's contact center has an annual volume of 36,000 and provides physician referral, event registration, service-line promotion and fulfillment, and community outreach.

Some may feel that this example is really an extension of marketing, but AtlantiCare Health System's vision is to build healthy communities. Its mission statement states, "AtlantiCare is an integrated system of services designed to help people achieve optimal health." This program is a reflection of the clinical philosophy of AtlantiCare, where president and CEO David P. Tilton says AtlantiCare wants to create an "epidemic of health" in southeastern New Jersey.[5]

In September 2007, the AtlantiCare contact center began working with the health system's community outreach team to provide a comprehensive approach to health screenings. Outreach screening programs include blood pressure, cholesterol, and glucose testing and are offered at various neighborhood events, such as monthly senior citizen meetings, church or community health fairs, and affinity groups. Previously, the community outreach team would attempt to follow up with the participants whose results were outside the normal range. However, the volume became burdensome and better documentation was required. This is where the contact center could provide a solution.

Case studies and best practices in clinical services integration

Contact center nurses place outreach calls to individuals who show blood pressure, cholesterol, or glucose levels outside the normal range of the American Heart Association guidelines. The nurse provides education based on participants' individual health needs and confirms whether they have followed up with their primary care physician. If they have not, the nurse offers assistance in setting up an appointment and offers to send educational literature. If the individual does not have a physician, the nurse can provide a referral and assist with scheduling an appointment.

All of the interactions are documented in the contact center's software system. Maureen Donzuso, contact center manager, indicates that 13%–17% of participants require a follow-up call, translating to an average of 65 outbound calls per month.

Determining your approach

I've just examined five providers, each with a different approach to integrating the clinical services of the organization into the contact center. So, how do you get your call center integrated with your hospital's clinical services?

First, you need to establish with senior leadership that this is one of the purposes of your organization's call center. Make the case for why it is. As previously stated, the ROI and the resources needed for providing clinical services are usually different when the call center enters into this type of service. You need to have done your homework to be sure everyone involved is supportive.

Chapter 8

Second, relationship-building is essential. The contact center manager needs to forge relationships with the various clinical leaders to build trust. The clinicians want to know that their programs are going to be supported at least as well as they could have done themselves, and the contact center manager needs to build this sense of confidence. This is done through acquiring the necessary knowledge, hiring and training staff members, resourcing properly, role-playing, competency testing, and working collaboratively with the clinical partners.

Third, ensure you have the proper resources. Before entering the clinical services arena, analyze the following aspects of your contact center:

- Staffing mix—e.g., do we need to add registered nurses?
- Staffing levels—e.g., do we need more staff members if a particular program is going to increase call volumes and lengths?
- Software tools—e.g., do we need triage protocols?
- Hours of operation—e.g., do we need to be open 24/7?

Do not let these questions scare you away from entering the world of clinical services. This is often where some of the most memorable moments are created for your organization's patients. They'll remember that someone cared enough to call them after they left your hospital. A worried mom notices when someone immediately answers the phone at 2 a.m. and can offer advice about her sick child. It makes a difference.

9

Moving beyond marketing into hospital operations: Touch points along the patient continuum

Chapter 9

Moving beyond marketing into hospital operations: Touch points along the patient continuum

Chapter 8 identified opportunities for contact centers to expand their reach into clinical service lines. This chapter will identify opportunities to connect the call center with hospital operations, which may be a more feasible expansion option. Depending on the scope, the service expansion may be able to be absorbed into existing call center operations without additional resources.

It is still important to ensure that moving beyond the marketing department is defined as a strategic direction of the call center, as it will have an effect on traditional return on investment measurements. Therefore, there needs to be an agreement with senior leadership with respect to the call center's expanded role.

Expansion isn't an experiment

One word of caution in any expansion of contact center services: Ensure the strategic alignment of the new service with the organization's operating strategy. It has been mentioned often that you need to secure senior leadership support

Chapter 9

for the purpose and services of the contact center, but you also need to make sure your call center is adequately staffed to meet the needs of your hospital. Although they may have the best of intentions, call center supervisors may commit to assisting different departments without being prepared to do so. Before call center managers agree to take on additional volume, they must make sure their unit has the resources for the additional calls—whether with existing staff members, assistance from the department requesting services, new hires, or process changes.

Without careful planning, expansion can have a detrimental effect on core services of the call center, and thus the organization's bottom line. For example, if call volume grows substantially with the addition of nonmarketing programs, but resources aren't adequate, this can lead to long call queues, increased call abandonment rates, and lost customers. Also, representatives may rush their calls when faced with high call volumes and the pressure to provide prompt service. In the case of physician referrals, this will have a negative effect on appointment scheduling for physician offices. You can see how nonmarketing initiatives may potentially lead to the contact center being counterproductive to its core services.

If expansion into hospital operations is strategically aligned, supported by senior management, and provided with proper resources, the contact center is an ideal partner for many initiatives. The types of hospital operations that can collaborate with call centers are only limited by the innovation of the teams involved and whether they are willing to work outside of organizational silos.

Helping patients beat traffic

BJC HealthCare, introduced in Chapter 2, has 13 hospitals in its system. Two of its major locations are in the heart of St. Louis, an area that, like many metropolitan areas, is experiencing the added traffic burdens brought on by major construction and the closure of a primary route leading to the hospital. Easy access to the healthcare system by consumers was a previously identified organizational strategy, so BJC and its academic partner, Washington University School of Medicine, decided to tackle this challenge by trying to ease the stress of patients faced with unexpected delays from traffic bottlenecks.

In addition to having daily information available on its Web site, including links to current travel information from the Missouri Department of Transportation, BJC's call center also serves as a resource to patients en route to an appointment. Drivers can call the contact center to find out up-to-the-minute information about the best route to take. In addition, the contact center representative will call the physician's office or the hospital department where the patient is going and ask for the appointment to be held if the patient is delayed.

Clearly, this initiative could be handled by each department, but providing customers with a single contact point staffed by individuals who are able to provide up-to-the-minute information enhances the customer service experience. It also relieves hospital operations from providing directions, which can be quite time-consuming. Through collaboration and planning, BJC identified a win-win for customers and operations.

Chapter 9

Emory helps its employees

Call center representatives are ideal for addressing access-related challenges, as they provide consumers with assistance in accessing the organization that they work for every day. Emory Healthcare, introduced in Chapter 2, found it was facing a perceived access challenge from a population often overlooked: its own employees.

It is easy to believe that employees of a healthcare organization should be able to comfortably navigate the system to secure their own physician appointments. However, Emory found there was a perception among employees that it was difficult to obtain an appointment with an Emory physician. To solve this problem, the organization created the Emory Employee Access Line. If an appointment is not available within a medically appropriate time frame for the employee's condition, the call may be escalated to the call center's registered nurse, who can provide additional assistance in scheduling an appointment.

Started in 2004, the program is offered to employees and their family members. Although not all calls need to be escalated, there have been 3,000 calls per year into the Emory Employee Access Line. Strategically, this contact point is aligned with Emory's goal to communicate that the organization cares about its employees and their health. Prior to this program's implementation, only 30% of employees insured through Emory's employer-sponsored health plans were scheduling appointments with Emory providers. That number has increased to more than 50%. This is another example where core competencies of the contact center—representative availability, advocacy for the customer, and facilitating access to the organization—were promoted to an audience that is sometimes taken for granted.

This initiative required collaboration between Emory human resources, communications, clinical sections, and the contact center for it to be successful. Human resources and communications needed to promote the program effectively to employees via orientation, annual benefits enrollment, and the company intranet to create awareness of the access line. Clinical sections needed to be flexible with schedules to accommodate employees needing appointments in a medically appropriate time frame. The contact center needed to deliver on the promise of facilitating access for the customer, in this case, the Emory employee. As with most successful endeavors, it is the collective efforts of all involved that yielded more than a 60% increase in employee appointments with Emory physicians.

A way to show strengths, weaknesses

Several years ago, I was involved with a call center where the representatives expressed frustration with trying to schedule appointments with physician offices. They would hear that an office was closed to a particular health plan or to new patients completely, that new appointments were not available for weeks or months, that offices were closed for lunch—when the call center was busiest—and an assortment of other barriers to scheduling appointments.

The representatives began documenting the date, physician practice, reason for the inability to schedule an appointment, and the final resolution of the consumer call. Each month, a summary report was prepared and provided to senior leadership. It eventually became a document that physician department chairs were requesting and individual physicians wanted to see about their own practices. One of the large group practices affiliated with the organization used the information in this report to aid in its recruiting and physician planning strategies.

A private practice gastroenterologist was on the report because her office had declined to schedule an appointment; the receptionist told callers that the physician was not accepting new patients. When the doctor called to follow up on the issue, she explained that she was, in fact, accepting new patients. Upon discussing this with her staff members, she learned they had decided among themselves that she was busy enough and did not need any new patients at that time. Until the report came to her, she had no prior knowledge that her pipeline to new patients had been cut off, even if it was with the best of intentions. Although I wouldn't consider this "mystery shopping," it did provide the organization with insight to the physician access issues that its patients were experiencing.

Mystery shopping

BJC and Sharp—introduced in Chapter 8—are two organizations that mystery shop for their respective healthcare systems to learn what their customers are

Moving beyond marketing into hospital operations: Touch points along the patient continuum

experiencing. Both conduct mystery shopping not only via the phone, but also on-site to evaluate the face-to-face patient experience.

Other industries have done this for years, hiring outside firms to complete audits at every organizational customer touch point. This is not feasible within healthcare, largely due to the nature of service being delivered. However, most healthcare access points can and should have this research done, as it provides valuable insight into the patient care experience. Consequently, organizations can reinforce and reward practices that demonstrate customer-focused care and change those that are not. As a result of mystery shopping, Sharp learned that it needed to address the increasing demand for cost transparency. This was solved by placing an employee in the patient financial services department who could handle hospital price inquiries.

A virtual front door

The last case study of this chapter features a highly integrated contact center in Chicago. It is sometimes easy to believe that only the big operations can take on the challenges of the integrated call center. However, the team at Swedish Covenant Hospital embodies a vital tenet of a successful call center operation—the "can do" attitude. Never allowing obstacles to become barriers, Rose Jeanfreau, director of patient access services at the Swedish Covenant call center, is quick to point out what her staff members will do next. But what they have accomplished already is no small feat.

Chapter 9

> **Swedish Covenant Hospital**
>
> Swedish Covenant Hospital is a comprehensive healthcare facility providing health and wellness services to the communities of Chicago's north and northwest sides. Swedish Covenant is a 330-bed, nonprofit, academic, and community hospital offering a range of medical programs, including cancer, cardiac, surgical, women's health, and emergency services. It has more than 550 physicians on its medical staff and 2,200 employees. The call center handles more than 62,000 calls annually, making it a great example of what is possible, even in a small call center. The Swedish Covenant Hospital call center provides:
>
> - Appointment scheduling for outpatient procedures
> - Preregistration
> - Insurance verification
> - Physician referral
> - Class and event registration for community education
> - Response management for marketing calls to action
>
> www.swedishcovenant.org

All of the representatives in the department are cross-trained to provide all of the services listed in the accompanying sidebar. By completing the scheduling and registration process over the phone, patients are able to proceed directly to the testing or therapy department when they arrive on the day of care. Patient data are also entered in the hospital's accounts receivable system by call center staff members prior to the day of service.

Swedish Covenant has stepped up its efforts to improve the preadmission process for obstetric patients. Whenever patients call for a prenatal class, birthing center tour, or breast feeding class, they are asked whether they have time to preregister over the phone. If not, an obstetric packet is sent via mail.

In addition, Swedish Covenant Hospital serves a diverse community, and its multicultural call center staff is reflective of this diverse population. The staff includes representatives who are able to speak the following languages:

- Spanish
- Bosnian
- Croatian
- Serbian
- Hindi
- Urdu
- Punjabi
- Korean
- Tagalog

By offering assistance in these languages, the organization has extended its commitment to provide simple access to healthcare with the customer in mind. The contact center is a virtual front door to Swedish Covenant Hospital—an organization that is a member of the Planetree Alliance, which stresses a commitment to patient-centered care.

Call center integration with hospital operations—when aligned with organizational strategy—creates winning partnerships. These partnerships offer the hands-on operations staff more time to provide face-to-face services. They also keep telephone and Internet-based interactions in the call center environment, where they can be handled effectively and efficiently by trained professionals.

Chapter 9

The call center can be well-positioned to present solutions to a hospital's business problems, but it takes relationships with operations colleagues, as well as being knowledgeable of the organization's strategic direction, challenges, and resource limitations.

10

Embrace transparency, empower your customers, and build your business

CHAPTER 10

Embrace transparency, empower your customers, and build your business

When interviewed for this book, call center leaders from across the country expressed that customers have increasing expectations of hospitals, including being engaged in the hospital experience. Customers want a personalized, concierge kind of experience that goes above and beyond the expectation of quality. They do not want their experience to be the way it has always been—or at least the way many perceive it has been—with long waits, lack of information, and inefficient systems. More and more, consumers are expressing their expectations and a willingness to change providers for greater flexibility and responsiveness (e.g., a physician who will communicate via e-mail or one with online appointment scheduling.)

Consumers are increasingly savvy about quality, price, and how to obtain information and quality scores for healthcare providers. Although the information available via the Internet may not always be clear or reliable, consumers are doing their research. They know what they want, and they expect healthcare providers to meet these needs.

CHAPTER 10

We've got the technology, and they know it

Electronic medical records (EMR) are among the more commonly discussed topics related to improving quality within healthcare. Customers are aware of EMRs and other technology that makes an office visit more convenient. They expect providers to use such systems; they don't want to have to repeat their medical histories each time they visit the same organization, nor do they want to repeat their list of medications to multiple staff members during a single admitting process. If they contact the call center to register for a class for newly diagnosed diabetic patients, they don't want to be asked for all of their demographic information when they were just discharged from the hospital two weeks prior.

Patients are often frustrated and disappointed when they have interacted with a hospital or doctor for years, and yet their relationship with these providers is more impersonal than their relationship with a national retailer. With technology now enabling better distribution of information, customers have raised their expectations.

More progress to make

Outside of the emergency room, the telephone is often the first human interaction people have with the healthcare system. The caller may be inquiring about one of the thousands of different general information topics, trying to schedule an appointment for one of your hospital's hundreds of services, or requesting that you transfer them to a loved-one's hospital room. But in each case, the opportunity exists to create a distinctive moment where your organization stands out from the competition—not necessarily by what was said, but in how it was said.

Call management services that are consistently outstanding create a competitive advantage for organizations. Service excellence is highly pursued by healthcare organizations and great strides have been made by many, but consumer needs have not been fulfilled. Consumers are still looking for more speed, convenience, and personalization across the entire healthcare continuum.

Map out the customer experience

A hospital's telephonic access points are its virtual front door—and a good place to begin well-thought-out customer contact mapping and mystery shopping. Doing so will allow you to see how many times callers are transferred or sent to voicemail, how long they are in queue, or how often they abandon the call. These statistics are essential to understanding customer experiences and may be an indicator of how many customers you may be losing because of a poor first experience.

According to a 2007 study by The Beryl Institute, 75% of individuals who abandon calls (hang up) do not call back.[6] When that formula is applied to different call types, it is easy to see that this situation affects more than just

Chapter 10

the consumer. Your organization may lose revenue opportunities because of a bad service experience, as many consumers will look to a competing hospital to fulfill their healthcare needs.

'Mega' call centers

Well-run call centers provide professional telephonic management of various call types, as well as data analysis to determine call volumes and patterns to ensure proper staffing. In talking with call center leaders, some brought up the idea of the consolidated, or "mega," call center to aid in the continued pursuit of customer service excellence. This idea has already started with some organizations. Swedish Covenant Hospital, which I wrote about in Chapter 9, has chosen to consolidate its marketing response management, physician referral, centralized scheduling, preregistration, and insurance verification departments into a single call center. This optimizes its call center management expertise and representative's professional skill set, while enhancing the customer experience by simplifying telephone access to the organization.

Technology and staffing to support call centers are expensive, particularly for 24/7 operations. The larger the call center, the greater the efficiency and lower the cost per call. Therefore, to the extent possible, cross-training of staff and consolidation of services into a single call center provides organizations not only with their greatest return on investment, but with their greatest opportunity for creating a consistent customer experience. This does not mean the call center needs to be housed in a single space, as technology enables multiple sites to function as a single unit. These sites can be located virtually anywhere—including remote agents working from their own homes. However, if hospitals have multiple call centers all investing in their own technology, it reduces opportunities for leveraging the investment. With capital funding at a premium, most hospitals can't afford a lack of collaboration.

Although the mega call center offers the greatest efficiencies mathematically, it is not always the best decision for an organization. Within an organization, there may be a 24/7 call center for information technology to receive calls from internal staff members with hardware/software/network–related issues. There may be a call center for consumer and patient services. And there may be another call center for billing and financial services. Could these three call centers be consolidated into a mega–call center? Perhaps two of three could be consolidated, or maybe from an organizational perspective it would be determined that none of them could be consolidated. However, all of them could take advantage of technology sharing. Services such as call recording, screen capture, and advanced ACD systems are technologies that, when shared between three departments, become much more feasible capital purchases than when they are being used by a single, stand-alone business unit.

Web integration

This same principle applies to another area where call center leaders see potential for expansion: Web integration. The ability to engage with customers via Web chat or click-to-call (using voice-over Internet protocol) further enhances and empowers an organization's ability to engage customers. This also requires technology, but, if disseminated among multiple groups, it maximizes the investment.

Chapter 10

When hospitals first began building Internet sites, there were assumptions that call centers would see declining call volumes—particularly marketing call centers. Hospitals' first Web sites were primarily electronic brochures that offered limited opportunity for customers to interact with the organization. Many believed that callers would turn to the Internet to find information before they picked up the phone. However, this has not been the experience of most call centers when all other factors remained unchanged (e.g., there was not a decline in marketing spend that affected call volume).

The Internet appears to be attracting a population that is different from those who have historically called the contact center. Although hospitals are moving toward more transactional sites, there are still relatively few that enable a patient to chat with a hospital representative online, click-to-call, or schedule appointments in real time.

Physician relations and the call center

As hospital marketing departments increasingly turn their attention to physicians as potential customers, there are more opportunities for physician relations and call center departments to work together. Physician referral, as one of the foundations of the marketing call center, is ultimately intended to produce revenue for the hospital, but that revenue isn't actually generated until a patient passes through a physician's office. Many new practicing physicians have found their hospital's physician referral service to be a primary source of new patients. This is not due to preferential treatment provided by the hospital, but because a new physician often has what an established practice does not have: access.

Same-day, evening, and weekend appointments are often building blocks for a new practice. Consumers with colds, the flu, or sore throats are looking for these types of appointments when they call a physician referral line. This access creates the opportunity for the physician to build a relationship with patients who are not aligned with another provider. This is just one example of a service provided by the call center that can be marketed to new and potential members of your hospital's medical staff.

Depending on the other services provided by the call center, there may be an entire portfolio to share with physicians. For example, pediatric after-hours triage service, physician consult lines, information on continuing medical education programs, and patient hospital transfers are just a few programs that will appeal to the physician audience. Nonmedical staff physicians may also be interested in some of these programs, as well as knowing about how communication is managed regarding referred patients—another possible contact center–enabled service.

Beyond direct contact with physicians, there is also the ability to share information via common databases, assist with tracking of physician interactions with various services, and identify any practice issues/complaints to provide proactive conflict resolution.

Physician leaders and medical groups may also be interested in a call center's ability to provide disease management services. Call center leaders across the country identified this as an area of growth when talking to me about the industry's future. With aging baby boomers and technology that enables

Chapter 10

remote-patient monitoring, contact centers are positioned to be central figures in assisting providers in managing their patient populations 24/7. Coupling the disease management experience with the increasing adoption of EMRs provides an optimal environment for providing patients with improved quality and a greater continuum of care, particularly when integrated with physician practices as highlighted in the Cleveland Clinic case study in Chapter 8.

Outside the hospital

Even outside agencies have started to recognize the resources of the hospital call center. A September 2007 report was prepared by Denver Health for the Agency for Healthcare Research and Quality, U.S. Department of Health and Human Services. In it, the nurse advice line (hospital call center) was one of several health call centers identified as an established and trusted community resource, helping people make informed decisions and care for themselves during health events specifically defined in the report (e.g., bioterrorism, pandemics, etc.). The author found that with proper training, information, and resources, health call centers can help minimize or alleviate the demands on the healthcare delivery system, enabling providers to assist those most in need. This full report can be accessed at *www.ahrq.gov*.[7]

Final thoughts

There are three thoughts I'd like to leave you with in closing:

1. If you do not have a contact center, seriously think about establishing one. A well-run call center will yield a positive return on investment and enhance the customer experience. If your organization is expending resources in advertising and marketing, it will be to your benefit to create a customer-oriented access point to enable the consumer to engage with your hospital.

2. If you have a contact center, build relationships with service line, hospital operations, and physician leaders to secure opportunities for integration of the contact center with clinical and operational initiatives. Providing clinicians and frontline staff members with exceptional telephonic patient management enables them to spend more time in face-to-face interactions and provides patients with expedited answers to their questions.

3. Keep yourself well-informed on your organization's strategic initiatives. Find ways to help your hospital improve its performance and sustain viability. Create an annual business plan for your call center that aligns with the organizational goals and create tactics designed to deliver an exceptional customer experience.

References

1. Gary Ahlquist, Charles Beever, Rick Edmunds, David G. Knott, PhD, "Consumer and Physician Readiness for a Retail Healthcare Market: Changing the Basis for Competition," 2007 Consumerism Survey Report, Booz Allen Hamilton.

2. "The Call Center as a Marketing Channel," Solucient, 2005.

3. www.landsend.com, 2008.

4. www.harley-davidson.com, 2008

5. www.atlanticare.org, 2008

6. "It's Not Just a Call, It's a Customer," The Beryl Institute, May 2007.

7. Bogdan, G.M., Scherger D.L., Seroka A.M., Watson J., Johnson M., "Adapting Community Call Centers for Crisis Support: A Model for Home-Based Care and Monitoring." Prepared by Denver Health, published by the Agency for Healthcare Research and Quality, September 2007.